MW00947033

THE
DIY PROTEIN BARS
- COOKBOOK -

48 Easy, Healthy, No-Bake Treats
That Taste Like Dessert, But
They're Packed With Protein!

Copyright © 2016 Jessica Stier

All rights reserved. No part of this book may be reproduced or transmitted, in any form or by any means, without consent from the author.

This book is intended as a reference only, not as a medical manual. It is not intended as a substitute for any professional medical advice, diagnosis or treatment that you may have been prescribed by your doctor. Every human being is incredibly unique, so what may "work" for one person may not necessarily "work" for you (and vice versa). Always seek the advice of a physician and registered dietician where appropriate.

Nutrition labels provided in this book were accurate at the time it went to press.

Milky Way®, Snickers® and Twix® are registered trademarks of Mars, Inc. Reese's®, Almond Joy®, Mounds®, Pay Day® and Take 5® are registered trademarks of The Hershey Company. Nutella® is a registered trademark of Ferro, SpA. Cherry Ripe® is a registered trademark of Cadbury, Ltd. All trademarks remain property of their respective holders, and are used only to directly describe the products referenced in this book. Any mention of specific companies in this book does not imply endorsement by the author.

Library of Congress Control Number: 2016913696
CreateSpace Independent Publishing Platform, North Charleston, SC

ISBN-13: 978-1535564984
ISBN-10: 1535564989

Third Edition

MOCHA

SEVEN SINS

RASPBERRY ALMOND

CHUBBY HUBBY

PUMPED UP

RED VELVET CAKE

CARROT CAKE (with Cream Cheese Frosting & Coconut Coating)

ORANGE CRANBERRY

WHITE CHOCOLATE
MACADAMIA COOKIE

POWERHOUSE

FIND ME ON SOCIAL MEDIA!

Make sure to use the hashtags **#DessertsWithBenefits** and **#DIYProteinBars!**

Facebook   www.facebook.com/DessertsWithBenefits
www.facebook.com/DIYProteinBarsCookbook

Twitter   @DWBenefits
@DIYProteinBars

Pinterest   www.pinterest.com/WithBenefits

Tumblr   www.DessertsWithBenefits.tumblr.com

Instagram   @DessertsWithBenefits

SnapChat   DWBenefits

Blog   www.DessertsWithBenefits.com

E-Mail   DessertsWithBenefits@gmail.com

DEDICATION

I wrote this cookbook for all the Desserts with Benefits® fans who have asked me to write one throughout the years that I've been blogging. With the heaping amount of support I've received along the way, the publishing experience can only be described as *extraordinary*.

With every comment, I am thankful.

With every email, I am touched.

With every shout-out, I am over the moon.

With every testimonial, I am eternally grateful.

With all the encouragement, my nerves poof into thin air.

The friendly online community that I am in inspires me more than words can ever describe. So THANK YOU! Thank you, my lovely blog readers. You are inspiring, uplifting, thoughtful, and kindhearted souls.

TABLE OF CONTENTS

DUO PROTEIN BARS
(pg. 77-78)

ALMOND BUTTER

SUPER GREENS

MO-TELLA

DEATH BY CHOCOLATE

DUO

BLUEBERRY MUFFIN

PEANUT BUTTER

MATCHA GREEN TEA ALMOND

ABOUT THE AUTHOR

Jessica Stier is the author, photographer and recipe developer behind the *DIY Protein Bars* cookbook, which was inspired by her healthy dessert recipe blog, Desserts with Benefits® (www.DessertsWithBenefits.com). She is a healthy dessert expert with an interest and a strong scholarly background in the fields of Nutrition and Dietetics (thanks, university!), but before college she was the complete opposite. I guess we should start from the beginning, shall we?

I was born and raised in a quiet, homey neighborhood in Calgary, Alberta, Canada. Like most kids, I ate whatever I pleased. I plowed my way through boxes of candy bars, jumbo-sized bags of chocolate goodies, and enough candy to fill dozens of Halloween trick-or-treat pumpkin baskets (i.e., enough sugar to make the most seasoned sugar fiend sick with a stomachache and candy hangover).

When my family uprooted to the United States, so did my sugar addiction. All the way to age eighteen, I ate poorly (understatement of the year?) and didn't exercise. I ate chocolate bars for breakfast (yes, I'm serious), a bag of chips, "fruit" snacks, and a carton of sugary chocolate milk for lunch (are you getting a sugar rush just by reading this?), and something else nutritionally deficient for dinner, like nachos or instant noodles. I brought so much candy to school that I was known as "Hershey Girl," "Sourpatch Girl," and even just plain old, "girl with candy."

After every meal, I felt gross and uncomfortable with a foggy brain, but I kept on eating the unhealthy foods I had always eaten. A diet like that seemed normal. My family ate like that, the kids at school ate like that, it tasted good... so, what's the problem?

Why change?

When I turned sixteen and got my first job at a pretzel joint in the local shopping mall, I gained a little bit of weight. And by "a little" I mean "a lot." Like, twelve pounds in three months. This was a huge shock to me. I never gained weight like that before despite my inadequate diet and sedentary lifestyle. I may have been on the thin side my entire life, but I was always "skinny-fat." A lot of jiggle on bones with no muscle whatsoever.

My solution? Oh, just buy those 100-calorie snack packs and (attempt to) stop eating a bajillion pretzels dunked in butter every time they began to look dry. Yeah, that didn't fly. The excess salt, the dangerous trans fats, the highly refined sugar, the artificial sweeteners... it just made me want more. *A lot more.* And I paid the price for it – I was an emotional roller coaster with crazy cravings, either trapped in a steady state of lethargy or stuck in an unstoppable yo-yoing between sugar rush and sugar crash.

I just wanted to be better... healthier.

With perfect timing, I graduated high school and was about to enter university – a brand new stage in life where I decided to *start over. Completely.* I chose to major in Nutritional Sciences, and this was one of the best decisions I have ever made. I learned everything under the sun about food, nutrition, and the human body. I finally came to terms with *my own body*, the reasons why I ate the way I did, and how I *should* be eating. Now, just a few years later, I have finally found the solution to achieving consistent energy levels, and I am satiated for a long period of time (no more of those "I-must-eat-that-entire-tray-of-brownies-ASAP" feelings). I have boosted my metabolism, put on lean muscle (~15 pounds), and have lost some fat (~10 pounds).

~~I lived for chocolate.~~ I *live* for chocolate.

Don't get me wrong, I still indulge. I have (and will *always* have) a serious passion for sweets! I have just learned how to make those sweets secretly healthy.

Enter, Desserts with Benefits®

My blog was born late at night on April 20th, 2011 as a serious procrastination technique to avoid studying for finals. I didn't post a recipe, but rather, a list of desserts that were on my "Baking Wishlist," along with dishes that I've made but had turned out unsuccessful. Healthy baking is a difficult thing to do! I don't use *sugar* (white granulated sugar, brown sugar, high fructose corn syrup, etc.), *artificial sweeteners* (aspartame, sucralose, etc.), *white flour* (all purpose flour, cake flour, pastry flour, bread flour, bleached flours, etc.), or *unhealthy fats* (hydrogenated shortening, margarine, genetically modified oils). I mean, anything can be made to taste good using all the wrong ingredients, but is it what your *body* wants? I don't want my desserts to give off the same repercussions that typical unhealthy desserts do (aka, bloating, headache, stomachache, nausea).

When I started blogging, I hoped to show people that healthy ingredients can indeed make a delicious cake, muffin, pastry, cookie, and so on.

I am happy to say that, with the hundreds of testimonials I've received, with the loyal Desserts with Benefits® fans who comment regularly, and with the thousands upon *thousands* of people around the world who have tried (and loved!) my recipes...

I have met that goal.

ABOUT THE COOKBOOK

DIY Protein Bars is a collection of 48 easy, healthy, homemade, no-bake treats that taste like dessert, but just happen to be *packed* with protein! And there are options for everyone. The recipes are (or can be easily made) gluten-free, dairy-free, soy-free and vegan... but you'd never know it. One bite of any protein bar in this cookbook and you'll be screaming, **"OH-MY-GOSH-this-is-so-freakin'-good-how-can-this-be-good-for-me?!?"**

runs around in circles with joy
(Yes, that will happen.)

These protein bars are so tasty and addicting you'll never buy store-bought again!

Every protein bar recipe contains complete proteins (they contain all the essential amino acids). Protein is essential for muscle growth, repair and maintenance, and it is also necessary for maintaining blood pressure, fluid balance, pH balance and electrolyte levels within the body. The amount of protein you need is unique to you, but for the average person, it is recommended that you consume .8-2 grams of protein per kg of body weight. Personally, though, I think this puts too much of an emphasis on getting enough protein rather than eating a balanced diet, so I like to go by this:

10-35% of calorie intake from *protein*
20-35% of calorie intake from *fat*
45-65% of calorie intake from *carbohydrates*

I like to have my protein bar recipes fall somewhere within these ranges, but we don't need to go all "Anal Retentive Chef" here (thanks, Saturday Night Live)! These recommended percentages have a pretty wide range, and depending on what stage you are in your life – whether you're an athlete or a vegan, whether you're a growing teen or a pregnant woman, etc. – you can modify these numbers to suit your needs. I always recommend meeting with a registered dietician if you need some help (they don't bite, I swear)!

Each recipe in this cookbook includes a nutrition label so you can see how many calories, grams of fat, carbohydrates, protein and fiber are in each serving. No matter what, though, there are options for everyone's nutritional preferences: sugar-free, refined sugar-free, cholesterol-free, low-calorie, low-sodium, high fiber and high protein. These recipes might be "free" of some stuff, but they sure aren't free of flavor!

Oh, and don't you worry, the fun doesn't stop there. Every recipe in this cookbook is all natural – no artificial sweeteners, no synthetic food dyes, no artificial food flavorings, no hydrogenated oils and no preservatives whatsoever. That list right there is *unheard* of when it comes to store-bought protein bars.

Let's all make the same, scratch that, *better* versions of store-bought protein bars right at home.

These protein bars are perfect for both pro and novice athletes. After an intense workout, they're the best reward for sweating like an animal, dealing with your exhausted muscles, and trying to control those damn *uncontrollable* jelly legs.

But that's not all. Protein bars aren't only for the workoutaholics.

Do you have a sweet tooth?

Did you just raise your hand? Then these protein bars are for you too. They taste like candy bars (seriously, just check out the Candy Bar Protein Bar section on pg. 59-80) but without all the excess calories, fat and sugar. These recipes are a total godsend for the health conscious dessert lovers out there (aka, YOU). If you occasionally crave (and when I say "occasionally," I really mean "incessantly") a big hunk of – for lack of a better word – *sugar in a wrapper*, make a batch of protein bars instead and you'll be happy as can be... no guilt involved.

PUMPED UP PROTEIN BARS
(pg. 61-62)

PANTRY STAPLES

THE PROTEIN POWDERS

Brown rice protein powder is often the main dry ingredient and *cannot* be omitted. It might be possible to substitute it with other vegan protein powders (such as hemp, pea or soy), but every brand is different so I can't vouch for any other powders. Whey, casein, and egg white protein powder will *not* work in place of the brown rice protein. You will get a sticky, gooey mess on your hands. Delicious sticky gooeyness, but difficult to make and impossible to slice.

Organic Brown Rice Protein Powder
Nearly all of the recipes in this cookbook use brown rice protein powder. It is hypoallergenic, sugar-free, gluten-free, dairy-free, nut-free, vegan and non-GMO. I use SunWarrior® Classic Protein in both Vanilla and Chocolate. I attempted these recipes with 2 cheaper brands but paid for it in the end – they made the grittiest, most unpleasant bars!

Organic Grass-Fed Whey Protein Powder
One recipe in this cookbook uses whey protein powder because it is widely available and it is perfect for people who aren't vegan or allergic to dairy. I buy whatever brand is cheapest, but also organic, grass-fed, non-GMO, and sugar-free.

NUT AND SEED BUTTERS

Nut and seed butters are used in every single recipe in this cookbook! They are full of healthy fats, fiber, and essential nutrients. While some are high in protein, they are *incomplete* proteins (lack essential amino acids) so they need to be paired with something else to create a *complete* protein, such as oats, beans, etc. Always use natural nut/seed butters *without* added sugar, salt and oil – the ingredient list should contain only one ingredient: the nut/seed itself! Slightly runny nut/seed butters are ideal for these recipes. If you can, buy organic. If you want to make nut/seed butters at home, see Getting Started on pg. xiv. If you are allergic to nuts, replace the nut butters with seed butters.

Nut Butters
- Raw *and* Roasted Almond Butter
- Roasted Cashew Butter
- Raw Coconut Butter
- Roasted Hazelnut Butter
- Roasted Macadamia Butter
- Natural Roasted Peanut Butter
- Roasted Pecan Butter
- Roasted Walnut Butter

Seed Butters
- Toasted Pumpkin Seed Butter
- Toasted Sunflower Seed Butter

THE FLOURS

Almond Flour
Almond flour is ground up unblanched almonds. I use Now Foods® almond flour.

Oat Flour
Oat flour is simply ground up oats. I use Bob's Red Mill® certified gluten-free oat flour because it's whole grain, finely ground, easy to use, has a great flavor and is safe for people with celiac disease. Oat flour is difficult to replace in these protein bars recipes because it absorbs moisture and binds the mixture, allowing the protein bars to firm up nicely in the fridge and not fall apart when you slice and hold them.

Coconut Flour
Coconut flour is ground up dried coconut. I use Nutiva® because it's gluten-free, organic, non-GMO and inexpensive (from Costco!). It has a mild sweet, coconut flavor. Coconut flour is difficult to replace because it provides a specific texture and absorbs so much liquid.

Peanut Flour
Peanut flour is a defatted flour made from ground peanuts. I use Protein Plus® roasted all-natural peanut flour, which is high-protein, reduced-fat and gluten-free. Peanut flour is difficult to replace because it absorbs moisture, binds the mixture, provides extra peanut flavor *and* a punch of protein. ¼ cup of peanut flour has 110 calories, 4g fat, 8g carbs, 4g fiber and 16g protein. ¼ cup of peanuts has 170 calories, 14g fat, 5g carbs, 2g fiber and 7g protein.

NON-DAIRY MILKS
I have nothing against dairy milk as long as it's organic, I just prefer to use non-dairy milk because it has a longer shelf-life and won't spoil if the bars happen to drop to room temperature.

Unsweetened Vanilla Almond Milk
I use Silk® unsweetened vanilla almond milk (30 calories per cup). You can find it in the refrigerated section. I find that it has the best taste and creamiest texture, and I like how it's non-GMO.

Unsweetened Vanilla Coconut Milk
I'm not a huge fan of coconut milk as I prefer the flavor of almond milk, although I must admit it's *suuuper* creamy. Hence, I don't have a favorite brand. I just borrowed (okay, *stole*) a few cartons from my sister's place to make these recipes... I have a feeling she won't be reading this (she's the kind of person who skips right to the recipe without reading the instructions) so please don't tell... *shhhh!*

... Unsweetened Vanilla Soy, Cashew, Hemp, and Rice Milk should work just fine too!
If using soymilk, always buy organic and non-GMO. Never conventional... ever.

CHOCOLATE

Chocolate... CHOCOLATE... CHOOOOCCCOLLAAATTEEE!! Yes. You will need chocolate to make some (ehem, a *lot*) of the recipes. This is what you'll need:

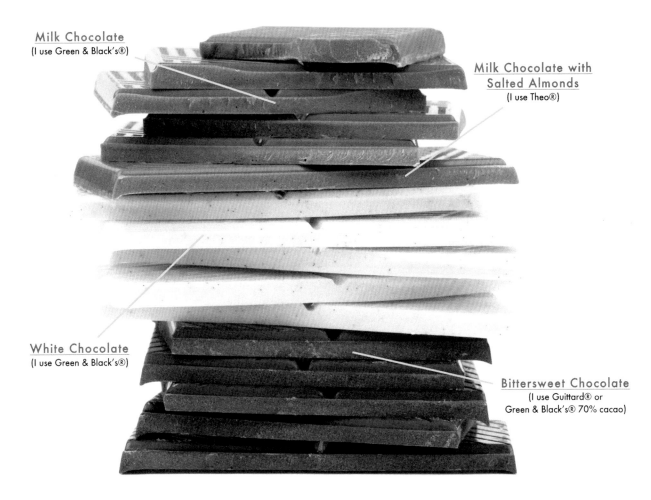

Milk Chocolate
(I use Green & Black's®)

Milk Chocolate with Salted Almonds
(I use Theo®)

White Chocolate
(I use Green & Black's®)

Bittersweet Chocolate
(I use Guittard® or Green & Black's® 70% cacao)

Mini Semi-Sweet Chocolate Chips (I use Enjoy Life®)

Cacao Nibs

Unsweetened Natural Cocoa Powder

Unsweetened Dutch Processed Cocoa Powder

Prefer to use no-sugar-added chocolate instead?

I like Lily's® and Coco Polo® sugar-free chocolate because they are both all-natural and non-GMO. Lily's is fair-trade too!

FLAVORINGS
Always use natural flavors. If available, use organic too

Extracts and Such
- Almond Extract (I use Simply Organic®)
- Banana Flavor (I use Bakto Flavors®)
- Blueberry Flavor (I use Bakto Flavors®)
- Butter Flavor (I use LorAnn Oils®* or Silver Cloud Estates®… I buy whichever is cheapest)

    *LorAnn Oils® sells a similar flavoring, the *Butter Vanilla Bakery Emulsion*, which contains hydrogenated oils! Only buy the *Butter Emulsion*, which is all-natural, trans fat-free, sugar-free, gluten-free and vegan.

- Butterscotch Flavor (I use Frontier Co-Op®)
- Cherry Flavor (I use Bakto Flavors®)
- Mint Flavor (I use Frontier Co-Op®)
- Raspberry Flavor (I use Bakto Flavors®)
- Strawberry Flavor (I use Bakto Flavors®)
- Vanilla Extract, Pure (I use homemade* but you can use Nielsen Massey® too)
- Vanilla Bean Paste (I use homemade* but you can use Nielsen Massey® too)

    *You can make Vanilla Extract and Vanilla Bean Paste at *home!* Just go to www.DessertsWithBenefits.com and in the search bar, type in: "Homemade Vanilla Extract" or "Homemade Vanilla Bean Paste"

Spices and Other Strong Flavors
- Ground Cinnamon
- Ground Nutmeg
- Espresso Powder
- Brewed Espresso (you can use decaf if you want)
- Salt (sometimes I use Pink Himalayan Salt instead)
- Flaked Sea Salt
- Rum (yes, rum)
- Alcohol-Free Liquid Chlorophyll Concentrate (I use ChlorOxygen®)
- Matcha Green Tea Powder (I use DōMatcha®)
- Original Amazing Grass® Amazing Meal® Powder

INGREDIENTS FOR FROSTINGS, COATINGS, TOPPINGS AND BASES

Protein bars are great and all, but they're so much better with some fun little extras. Like a nice chocolate shell. Or maybe even a chocolate Greek yogurt frosting. Oh, and some sprinkles too!

Plain, Nonfat Greek Yogurt

Always buy plain, unsweetened yogurt to avoid the added sugar, food dyes and other additives. Get organic to avoid the added hormones, antibiotics, steroids, etc.

Neufchâtel Cream Cheese

If you can't find Neufchâtel, just use ⅓ Less Fat Cream Cheese (they're basically the same thing).

Mascarpone

I haven't been able to find organic Mascarpone, but I buy mine from Whole Foods Market® because I trust their products more than the typical grocery store products.

Coconut Oil

Unrefined coconut oil has a strong coconut flavor while refined coconut oil is neutral. Choose whichever kind you want, just make sure it's non-hydrogenated!

Roasted Almonds, Peanuts, Pecans, Pumpkin Seeds and Hulled Sunflower Seeds

Caramel Sauce

I use Date Lady® Organic Caramel Sauce because it contains no added sugar (it's made from dates)! Another brand I like is Hot Cakes®.

> You can also make Caramel Sauce *at home*! Go to www.DessertsWithBenefits.com and in the search bar, type in: "Homemade Caramel Sauce"

100% Fruit Spread (no sugar added)

I use St. Dalfour® or Nature's Hollow in strawberry, but you can use whatever flavor you want!

Psyllium Husk Powder

I use Now Foods® psyllium husk powder. Be sure to use the *powder* and not the whole psyllium husks.

Ground Flaxseed Meal

I use Bob's Red Mill® whole ground flaxseed meal.

Natural Rainbow Sprinkles

I use India Tree® natural rainbow sprinkles.

Reduced Fat Unsweetened Shredded Coconut
I use Let's Do...Organic® shredded coconut because it's organic and contains no added sugar.

Graham Crackers
When I make protein bars for myself, I use Mi-Del® 100% whole wheat honey grahams. When I make protein bars for anyone with a gluten allergy or with celiac disease, I use S'moreables®. The nutrition facts for recipes containing graham crackers are calculated using Mi-Del® 100% whole wheat honey grahams.

Pretzel Rods
I've used quite a few different kinds of pretzel rods and pretzel sticks, including Mary's Gone Crackers® sea salt pretzel sticks (organic, whole grain, and gluten-free), Newman's Own® salted pretzel rods (organic), and grocery store brand pretzel sticks. I think the pretzel rods are best because they stay the crunchiest the longest. The nutrition facts for recipes containing pretzel rods are calculated using Newman's Own® salted pretzel rods.

All-Natural Vanilla Marshmallows
I use Dandies® all-natural vegan vanilla marshmallows.

Garbanzo Beans/Chickpeas
I use canned chickpeas because, to be honest, cooking them takes way too long. Use unsalted chickpeas if you can find it!

Crispy Brown Rice Cereal
I use Erewhon® because it's organic, gluten-free and whole-grain.

Quick-Cooking Oats
I use Bob's Red Mill® certified gluten-free quick-cooking oats.

Quinoa Flakes
I use Ancient Harvest® quinoa flakes.

NATURAL SWEETENERS

Liquid Stevia Extract
Stevia is an all-natural, calorie-free, sugar-free sweetener (derived from the Stevia rebaudiana herb) that does not affect blood glucose levels. It's 300x sweeter than sugar, so it's really easy to use too much, causing the dish you're making to taste bitter. I use SweetLeaf® because it tastes great and it's organic. In this book, I use the following flavors:
- Stevia Clear/Plain
- Vanilla Crème
- Coconut
- English Toffee

Another brand I sometimes use is NuNaturals®. *Always* use alcohol-free stevia.

Honey
I use Nature Nate's® 100% Pure Raw & Unfiltered Honey. It looks similar to the honey you'll find in those bear-shaped bottles but is just slightly thicker and *much* tastier!

Pure Maple Syrup
Never use the artificial stuff – it's just high-fructose corn syrup blended with artificial flavors, dyes, preservatives, and all that sorta crappy crap crapola! Pure maple syrup is smooth, luxurious and *packed* with flavor (and nutrients)!

FRUITS AND VEGETABLES
Fruits and vegetables are used in quite a few recipes. They provide natural sweetness (without having to add sugar), along with some fiber, vitamins and minerals. Always seek organic and non-GMO fruits and veggies with *no* added sugar.

Fresh
- Beets
- Carrots
- Lemons
- Oranges
- Baby Spinach

Prepackaged and Canned
- Unsweetened Applesauce
- Beets (just the juice, it's nature's food dye!)
- 100% Pure Pumpkin Puree

Dried
- Dried Unsweetened Blueberries
- Dried Unsweetened Cranberries
- Unsweetened Raisins

Freeze-Dried
- Freeze-Dried Bananas
- Freeze-Dried Cherries
- Freeze-Dried Raspberries
- Freeze-Dried Strawberries

ESSENTIAL KITCHEN TOOLS

KITCHEN WEIGH SCALE (a must must *must!*)
I make every single recipe using a kitchen scale. In my kitchen, a scale is more important than measuring cups. In the recipes, I start off each ingredient by weight, and then in parentheses, the estimated equivalent in volume. Weighing your ingredients is much more accurate than measuring ingredients with measuring cups. 1 cup of Oat Flour will weigh about 120g sifted, or 180g packed... that is a huge difference that will lead to an even bigger difference in taste, texture and appearance. So stick with the scale!
I use my Escali® Arti Glass Kitchen Scale.

ELECTRIC STAND MIXER WITH BEATER ATTACHMENT (or super buff biceps)
Nearly every recipe in this cookbook uses an electric stand mixer. It mixes the dough thoroughly, quickly and easily.
You can certainly do without the stand mixer and mix everything by hand, but just know that going that route will take 5x as long (and about 10x more patience).
I use my KitchenAid® Artisan® Series 5-Quart Tilt-Head Stand Mixer.

SMALL FOOD PROCESSOR
You'll need this to blend certain ingredients (like freeze-dried fruit), and if you make your own oat flour from rolled oats (certified gluten-free if necessary). I just buy my oat flour because it's finely ground, it's easy to use, it has great flavor and it is safe for people with celiac disease.
I use my Cuisinart® Mini-Prep® Plus Food Processor.

MIXING BOWLS
Have small-, medium- and large-sized bowls.

MEASURING SPOONS
Have ⅛ tsp, ¼ tsp, ½ tsp, ¾ tsp, 1 tsp and 1 tbs.

MEASURING CUPS
Have ¼ cup, ⅓ cup, ½ cup and 1 cup.

SPOONS, FORKS, AND A SHARP 9-10" KNIFE

2½" OR 2¾" CIRCLE COOKIE CUTTER

FINE-MESH SIEVE

WIRE WHISKS AND SILICONE SPATULAS

8X8" AND 9X9" SQUARE BROWNIE PANS

JELLY ROLL PAN WITH A FITTING SILICONE BAKING MAT

I use a 13x18" jelly roll pan and 11⅝"x16½" Silpat®

PASTRY ROLLER

This just makes your life a little easier when you press the protein bar "dough" in the pan.

MICROPLANE AND GRATER

To zest oranges and lemons and to grate carrots.

CAKE PEDESTAL AND CAKE DOME

You'll need this to store protein bars with frostings since you can't wrap those in sandwich baggies.

PLASTIC WRAP AND PLASTIC SANDWICH BAGGIES

PRE-CUT PARCHMENT BAKING SHEETS (12½X16")

I use If You Care® compostable, unbleached, chlorine-free parchment baking paper.

DOUBLE BOILER

You'll need this to melt chocolate... lots and lots of lovely chocolate!
I use my Farberware® 2-Quart Covered Double Boiler. It's perfect for all types of chocolate – white chocolate, milk chocolate and dark chocolate!

GETTING STARTED

HOW MUCH WILL THESE DIY PROTEIN BARS COST ME?

Are you ready for a surprise? Seriously, you ready?

Despite the *seemingly* expensive ingredients used in this cookbook, DIY protein bars are actually *less expensive* than store-bought protein bars. All you need to do is shop around (most often online, from Amazon.com, ThriveMarket.com and iHerb.com) for the best prices, find some coupons, use a discount code, and then say "KA-CHING!"

It also helps if you make your nut and seed butters at home. Just go to www.DessertsWithBenefits.com and in the search bar, type in "Raw Pecan Butter" – the process of making your own nut/seed butter is the same for all nuts/seeds. Just swap the pecans in the recipe with whatever nut/seed you need!

STORE-BOUGHT PROTEIN BARS:

Quest® Chocolate Brownie Protein Bar — **$2.79**

Pure Protein® Chocolate Deluxe Protein Bar — **$2.99**

PowerBar® Chocolate Brownie Protein Bar — **$2.99**

MET-Rx® Chocolate Fudge Deluxe Protein Bar — **$2.63**

DIY PROTEIN BARS:

$0.99	½ cup Roasted Almond Butter
$0.38	1 cup + 2 tbs Unsweetened Vanilla Almond Milk
$0.68	1 tsp Vanilla Crème-Flavored Liquid Stevia Extract
$7.17	1¼ cups Chocolate Brown Rice Protein Powder
$0.66	⅔ cup Oat Flour
$0.25	2 tbs Unsweetened Natural Cocoa Powder
$0.00	⅛ tsp Salt
$0.44	2 tbs Mini Semi-Sweet Chocolate Chips

$10.57 (cost of the entire batch)

÷ 10 BARS

$1.06 (cost of a single bar)

That means you can save up to **$1.93** PER protein bar!

Prices are obtained from the products' websites and/or Amazon.com (prices vary on Amazon.com and are subject to change). The DIY Protein Bar cost is calculated using the Chocolate Protein Bar recipe (pg. 1) and the ingredients from Pantry Staples (pg. v-xi).

HOW TO LINE YOUR BROWNIE PAN

1. Cut your parchment paper into long strips so that it fits nicely inside your pan. The majority of the recipes in this cookbook call for an 8x8" brownie pan, so you'll need to cut the parchment paper into strips slightly thinner than the size of the pan – about 7½" (if you are using the same pre-cut sheets that I use, simply fold the paper in half widthwise and cut about 1" off the creased side).

2. Place the paper inside the pan, leaving the overhang for easy removal later on. Feel free to use mini binder clips on the sides of the pan to keep the paper in place. This makes it easier to spread and flatten the protein dough inside the pan.

HOW TO MAKE PICTURE-PERFECT PROTEIN BARS

Complete steps 1 and 2 on the previous page, then proceed with the following steps:

3. Make the protein bar recipe and scoop the mixture into the pan.

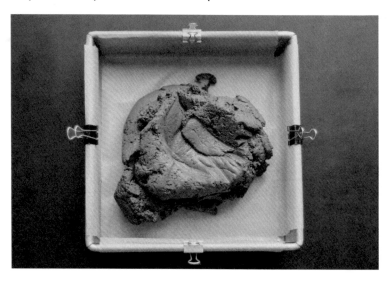

4. Use a silicone spatula to press down on the mixture and spread it to the edges of the pan (pictured on the left). If you want perfectly even protein bars, use a pastry roller after the spatula (pictured on the right).

5. Fold one side of the parchment paper overhang over the flattened protein bars and use your finger to round out the edges. Run your finger along the edge until it's smooth. Do this on all four sides.

6. Tightly cover the pan with plastic wrap and refrigerate overnight.
7. The next day, remove the protein bars from the pan. Using a sharp 9-10" knife, slice the mixture down the center and rotate. To slice into 10 bars, each protein bar should be around 1½". To slice into 12 bars, slice the mixture down the center again to make a + sign, then slice each square into three long, thin bars.

HOW TO MELT CHOCOLATE AND COAT YOUR PROTEIN BARS WITH IT

1. Fill the bottom portion of the double boiler with 2-3" of water. Make sure the water doesn't touch the bottom of the double boiler insert! Place the double boiler over medium heat.
2. While the water is heating up, break the chocolate into chunks and place inside the double boiler insert. When the water starts to simmer, reduce the heat to medium-low.
3. Stir occasionally until the chocolate is melted and completely smooth.

4. Place a silicone baking mat on top of a jelly roll pan and line the protein bars on top.

**RED VELVET CAKE
PROTEIN BARS**
(pg. 27-28)

5. With a large spoon (I use a tablespoon measuring spoon), ladle the chocolate over the protein bars. Try to encase the entire protein bar with chocolate, but it doesn't have to be perfect.

6. Refrigerate until firm (~1 hour). Individually wrap the protein bars in plastic sandwich baggies and refrigerate to store.

Buuut they're really good right now. So you should totally snack on them. Right now. Ehem...

FINALLY ABOUT TO MAKE A RECIPE? BEFORE YOU DO, READ THIS!

Just as a precaution, *always* read through the entire recipe once or twice from start to finish before diving in and making some protein bars. Cooking on the fly can lead to some serious kitchen fails (trust me, I've come across every hitch imaginable by cooking without reading the instructions first).

rolls eyes

But I've learned my lesson. I've learned to avoid substituting and omitting ingredients because 99% of the time, it will not work. You will be sad. So sad. The recipes here are tried and true so we can love them the way they are.

Brown rice protein powder is the main dry ingredient and *cannot* be omitted. It might be possible to substitute it with other vegan protein powders (such as hemp, pea or soy), but every brand is different so I can't vouch for any other types of powders. All I know is that whey protein powder, casein protein powder and egg white protein powder will *not* replace the brown rice protein powder.

Good news! There is one exception to this rule. The liquid stevia extract used in these recipes can be replaced with all-natural packeted sweeteners, such as organic stevia, Truvia®, Stevia in the Raw®, etc. Check out the www.DessertsWithBenefits.com FAQ page for a Sweetener Conversion Chart!

TIME-SAVING TIP
Use a kitchen scale! In the Essential Kitchen Tools section on pg. xii, I talk about how I use a kitchen scale to make all of my recipes. A scale helps you measure the ingredients properly so you get the same final product every time you make a recipe. Although, accuracy isn't a scale's only purpose. Using a scale allows you to make accurate nutrition labels (or simply calculate the correct number of calories, fat, carbs, protein, etc.). You also use less cooking materials, from mixing bowls to utensils to measuring cups to measuring spoons. Less dishes to wash? Yes, please. Because that gives us more time to eat.

PROTEIN BAR STORAGE TIPS
All protein bars keep for ~1 week in the fridge and can also be frozen for up to 3-4 months. To freeze, place the protein bars in plastic sandwich baggies, seal tightly, and place in the freezer door. If you want to freeze bars that have frosting, like the Birthday Cake Protein Bars (pg. 33-34), put the bars on a sheet of parchment paper on top of a plate, then place in the freezer *uncovered* for 2 hours. Place the frozen solid bars in sandwich baggies. To thaw, simply leave the frozen protein bars in the fridge overnight, or, leave at room temperature for ~2 hours.

If you have any other questions, feel free to ask me on my blog: www.DessertsWithBenefits.com

Okay, that's it. Now go make some healthy protein bars! *fist pump*

ORIGINAL FLAVORS

CHOCOLATE PROTEIN BARS

Yield: 10 Protein Bars

128g (½ cup) Roasted Almond Butter (Natural Roasted Peanut Butter works great too!)
1 cup + 2 tablespoons Unsweetened Vanilla Almond Milk
1 teaspoon Vanilla Crème-Flavored Liquid Stevia Extract
168g (1¼ cups, lightly packed) Chocolate Brown Rice Protein Powder
80g (⅔ cup) Oat Flour
2 tablespoons Unsweetened Natural Cocoa Powder
⅛ teaspoon Salt
2 tablespoons Mini Semi-Sweet Chocolate Chips

① Line an 8x8" brownie pan with parchment paper. Set aside.
② In an electric stand mixer bowl fitted with a beater attachment, add all of the ingredients except the mini chocolate chips. Mix on low speed until everything is fully incorporated.
③ Scrape down the sides of the bowl. Mix on medium speed for one last mix. Mixture should be thick and fudgy, like cookie dough.
④ Scoop the mixture into the brownie pan and flatten it out. Sprinkle the mini chocolate chips on top and press them into the surface. Tightly cover the pan with plastic wrap and refrigerate overnight.
⑤ Lift the mixture out of the pan. Slice into 10 bars. Individually wrap the protein bars in plastic sandwich baggies and refrigerate to store (keeps for ~1 week).

Nutrition Facts

Serving Size 1 Chocolate Protein Bar (68g)

Amount Per Serving	
Calories 190	Calories from Fat 80
	%Daily Value*
Total Fat 8g	**13%**
Saturated Fat 1g	**6%**
Trans Fat 0g	
Cholesterol 0mg	**0%**
Sodium 85mg	**3%**
Total Carbohydrate 12g	**4%**
Dietary Fiber 4g	**17%**
Sugars 2g	
Protein 17g	
Vitamin A 0%	Vitamin C 0%
Calcium 15%	Iron 20%

PEANUT BUTTER PROTEIN BARS

Yield: 10 Protein Bars

128g (½ cup) Natural Roasted Peanut Butter
1 cup + 3 tablespoons Unsweetened Vanilla Almond Milk
1 teaspoon Vanilla Crème-Flavored Liquid Stevia Extract
168g (1¼ cups, lightly packed) Vanilla Brown Rice Protein Powder
90g (¾ cup) Peanut Flour
¼ teaspoon Salt
2 tablespoons Peanuts, chopped

Nutrition Facts

Serving Size 1 Peanut Butter Protein Bar (72g)

Amount Per Serving

Calories 190	Calories from Fat 80

	%Daily Value*
Total Fat 9g	14%
Saturated Fat 1g	5%
Trans Fat 0g	
Cholesterol 0mg	0%
Sodium 115mg	5%
Total Carbohydrate 9g	3%
Dietary Fiber 4g	16%
Sugars 2g	
Protein 21g	

Vitamin A 0%	•	Vitamin C 0%
Calcium 10%	•	Iron 15%

① Line an 8x8" brownie pan with parchment paper. Set aside.
② In an electric stand mixer bowl fitted with a beater attachment, add all of the ingredients except for the chopped peanuts. Mix on low speed until everything is fully incorporated.
③ Scrape down the sides of the bowl and add the chopped peanuts. Mix on medium speed for one last mix. Mixture should be thick and fudgy, like cookie dough.
④ Scoop the mixture into the brownie pan and flatten it out. Tightly cover the pan with plastic wrap and refrigerate overnight.
⑤ Lift the mixture out of the pan. Slice into 10 bars. Individually wrap the protein bars in plastic sandwich baggies and refrigerate to store (keeps for ~1 week).

ALMOND BUTTER PROTEIN BARS

Yield: 10 Protein Bars

128g (½ cup) Roasted Almond Butter
1 cup Unsweetened Vanilla Almond Milk
1 teaspoon Vanilla Crème-Flavored Liquid Stevia Extract
1 teaspoon Almond Extract
168g (1¼ cups, lightly packed) Vanilla Brown Rice Protein Powder
48g (½ cup) Almond Flour
30g (¼ cup) Oat Flour
¼ teaspoon Salt
2 tablespoons Roasted Almonds, chopped

Nutrition Facts	
Serving Size 1 Almond Butter Protein Bar (63g)	
Amount Per Serving	
Calories 190	Calories from Fat 90
	%Daily Value*
Total Fat 10g	15%
Saturated Fat 0.5g	4%
Trans Fat 0g	
Cholesterol 0mg	0%
Sodium 120mg	5%
Total Carbohydrate 8g	3%
Dietary Fiber 4g	15%
Sugars < 1g	
Protein 17g	
Vitamin A 0% •	Vitamin C 0%
Calcium 10% •	Iron 15%

① Line an 8x8" brownie pan with parchment paper. Set aside.
② In an electric stand mixer bowl fitted with a beater attachment, add all of the ingredients. Mix on low speed until everything is fully incorporated.
③ Scrape down the sides of the bowl. Mix on medium speed for one last mix. Mixture should be thick and fudgy, like cookie dough.
④ Scoop the mixture into the brownie pan and flatten it out. Sprinkle the chopped almonds on top and press them into the surface. Tightly cover the pan with plastic wrap and refrigerate overnight.
⑤ Lift the mixture out of the pan. Slice into 10 bars. Individually wrap the protein bars in plastic sandwich baggies and refrigerate to store (keeps for ~1 week).

COCONUT PROTEIN BARS

Yield: 10 Protein Bars

128g (½ cup) Raw Coconut Butter, melted
1 cup + 2 tablespoons Unsweetened Vanilla Coconut Milk, room temperature
1 teaspoon Coconut-Flavored Liquid Stevia Extract
168g (1¼ cups, lightly packed) Vanilla Brown Rice Protein Powder
36g (¼ cup) Coconut Flour
⅛ teaspoon Salt
2 tablespoons Reduced Fat Unsweetened Shredded Coconut

① Line an 8x8" brownie pan with parchment paper. Set aside.
② In an electric stand mixer bowl fitted with a beater attachment, add the melted coconut butter, coconut milk and stevia extract. Mix on low speed while you prepare the dry ingredients.
③ In a medium-sized mixing bowl, whisk together the protein powder, coconut flour and salt. Turn off the stand mixer and dump in the dry ingredients. Return mixer to low speed and mix until the dry ingredients are fully incorporated. Scrape down the sides of the bowl if necessary. Mixture should be thick and fudgy, like cookie dough.
④ Scoop the mixture into the brownie pan and flatten it out. Sprinkle the shredded coconut on top and press it into the surface. Tightly cover the pan with plastic wrap and refrigerate overnight.
⑤ Lift the mixture out of the pan and let it sit on the counter for 10 minutes to soften. Slice into 10 bars. Individually wrap the protein bars in plastic sandwich baggies and refrigerate to store (keeps for ~1 week).

Nutrition Facts

Serving Size 1 Coconut Protein Bar (62g)

Amount Per Serving	
Calories 170	Calories from Fat 80
	%Daily Value*
Total Fat 8g	**13%**
Saturated Fat 7.5g	**38%**
Trans Fat 0g	
Cholesterol 0mg	**0%**
Sodium 85mg	**3%**
Total Carbohydrate 9g	**2%**
Dietary Fiber 5g	**22%**
Sugars 2g	
Protein 14g	
Vitamin A 0% •	Vitamin C 0%
Calcium 6% •	Iron 10%

SUNFLOWER SEED PROTEIN BARS

Yield: 10 Protein Bars

Nutrition Facts	
Serving Size 1 Sunflower Seed Butter Protein Bar (68g)	
Amount Per Serving	
Calories 190	Calories from Fat 80
	%Daily Value*
Total Fat 9g	**14%**
Saturated Fat 1g	**5%**
Trans Fat 0g	
Cholesterol 0mg	**0%**
Sodium 130mg	**6%**
Total Carbohydrate 11g	**4%**
Dietary Fiber 3g	**13%**
Sugars 1g	
Protein 16g	
Vitamin A 0% •	Vitamin C 0%
Calcium 10% •	Iron 15%

128g (½ cup) Toasted Sunflower Seed Butter
1 cup + 2 tablespoons Unsweetened Vanilla Almond Milk
1 teaspoon Vanilla Crème-Flavored Liquid Stevia Extract
168g (1¼ cups, lightly packed) Vanilla Brown Rice Protein Powder
80g (⅔ cup) Oat Flour
¼ teaspoon Salt
1 tablespoon Hulled Sunflower Seeds

① Line an 8x8" brownie pan with parchment paper. Set aside.
② In an electric stand mixer bowl fitted with a beater attachment, add the sunflower seed butter, almond milk and stevia extract. Mix on low speed while you prepare the dry ingredients.
③ In a medium-sized mixing bowl, whisk together the protein powder, oat flour and salt. Turn off the stand mixer and dump in the dry ingredients. Return mixer to low speed and mix until the dry ingredients are fully incorporated. Scrape down the sides of the bowl if necessary. Mixture should be thick and fudgy, like cookie dough.
④ Scoop the mixture into the brownie pan and flatten it out. Sprinkle the sunflower seeds on top and press them into the surface. Tightly cover the pan with plastic wrap and refrigerate overnight.
⑤ Lift the mixture out of the pan. Slice into 10 bars. Individually wrap the protein bars in plastic sandwich baggies and refrigerate to store (keeps for ~1 week).

PUMPKIN SEED PROTEIN BARS

Yield: 10 Protein Bars

128g (½ cup) Toasted Pumpkin Seed Butter
1 cup + 2 tablespoons Unsweetened Vanilla Almond Milk
1 teaspoon Vanilla Crème-Flavored Liquid Stevia Extract
168g (1¼ cups, lightly packed) Vanilla Brown Rice Protein Powder
80g (⅔ cup) Oat Flour
⅛ teaspoon Salt
2 tablespoons Toasted Pumpkin Seeds, chopped

Nutrition Facts	
Serving Size 1 Pumpkin Seed Protein Bar (66g)	
Amount Per Serving	
Calories 180	Calories from Fat 70
	%Daily Value*
Total Fat 8g	**12%**
Saturated Fat 1.5g	**7%**
Trans Fat 0g	
Cholesterol 0mg	**0%**
Sodium 95mg	**4%**
Total Carbohydrate 11g	**4%**
Dietary Fiber 3g	**13%**
Sugars < 1g	
Protein 17g	
Vitamin A 2% • Vitamin C 0%	
Calcium 6% • Iron 20%	

① Line an 8x8" brownie pan with parchment paper. Set aside.

② In an electric stand mixer bowl fitted with a beater attachment, add the pumpkin seed butter, almond milk and stevia extract. Mix on low speed while you prepare the dry ingredients.

③ In a medium-sized mixing bowl, whisk together the protein powder, oat flour and salt. Turn off the stand mixer and dump in the dry ingredients. Return mixer to low speed and mix until the dry ingredients are fully incorporated. Scrape down the sides of the bowl if necessary. Mixture should be thick and fudgy, like cookie dough.

④ Scoop the mixture into the brownie pan and flatten it out. Sprinkle the pumpkin seeds on top and press them into the surface. Tightly cover the pan with plastic wrap and refrigerate overnight.

⑤ Lift the mixture out of the pan. Slice into 10 bars. Individually wrap the protein bars in plastic sandwich baggies and refrigerate to store (keeps for ~1 week).

PROTEIN POWDER-FREE PROTEIN BARS

Yield: 12 Protein Bars

200g (1¾ cups) Quick-Cooking Oats
56g (½ cup) Ground Flaxseed Meal
2 teaspoons Ground Cinnamon
¼ teaspoon Salt
15oz can Garbanzo Beans/Chickpeas (unseasoned)
245g (1 cup) Unsweetened Applesauce
210g (1½ cups) Raisins
128g (½ cup) Natural Roasted Peanut Butter
1 tablespoon Pure Vanilla Extract

① Line a 9x9" brownie pan with parchment paper. Set aside.
② In a food processor, add the quick-cooking oats and blend until flour-like. Add the oat flour to an electric stand mixer bowl fitted with a beater attachment, along with the ground flaxseed meal, cinnamon and salt.
③ Drain the can of garbanzo beans and pour the beans into a sieve. Rinse *well* and drain off excess water (should yield 1½ cups).
④ In the food processor, add the garbanzo beans, applesauce, raisins, peanut butter and vanilla extract. Blend until smooth (you don't wanna chomp down on a whole chickpea!). Scoop the entire mixture into the stand mixer bowl. Turn the mixer on low speed. Mix until the ingredients are fully incorporated. Let the dough sit for 10 minutes.
⑤ Scoop the mixture into the brownie pan and flatten it out. Tightly cover the pan with plastic wrap and refrigerate overnight.
⑥ Lift the mixture out of the pan. Slice into 12 bars. Individually wrap the protein bars in plastic sandwich baggies and refrigerate to store (keeps for ~1 week).

Nutrition Facts

Serving Size 1 Protein Powder-Free Protein Bar (91g)

Amount Per Serving	
Calories 240	Calories from Fat 80
	%Daily Value*
Total Fat 9g	**13%**
Saturated Fat 1g	**4%**
Trans Fat 0g	
Cholesterol 0mg	**0%**
Sodium 55mg	**2%**
Total Carbohydrate 34g	**11%**
Dietary Fiber 6g	**23%**
Sugars 15g	
Protein 8g	
Vitamin A 0%	Vitamin C 4%
Calcium 4%	Iron 10%

MORE NUTTY FLAVOR IDEAS
Follow the Sunflower Seed Butter Fudge Protein Bars recipe and...

Brazil Nut Butter Protein Bars
... swap the Sunflower Seed Butter with Roasted Brazil Nut Butter!

Cashew Butter Protein Bars
... swap the Sunflower Seed Butter with Roasted Cashew Butter!

Pecan Butter Protein Bars
... swap the Sunflower Seed Butter with Roasted Pecan Butter! Feel free to add some spices (like cinnamon and nutmeg) and replace 2 tablespoons of almond milk with pure maple syrup.

Pistachio Butter Protein Bars
... swap the Sunflower Seed Butter with Raw or Roasted Pistachio Butter!

Macadamia Nut Butter Protein Bars
... swap the Sunflower Seed Butter with Roasted Macadamia Butter!

Walnut Butter Protein Bars
... swap the Sunflower Seed Butter with Roasted Walnut Butter! Feel free to add some spices (like cinnamon and nutmeg) and replace 2 tablespoons of almond milk with pure maple syrup.

SOME SEED-EATER FLAVOR IDEAS
If you have nut allergies, swap the nut butter in the recipe with a seed butter of your choice, and use your favorite nut-free milk to replace the almond milk! Follow the Sunflower Seed Butter Fudge Protein Bars recipe and...

Hemp Seed Butter Protein Bars
... swap the Sunflower Seed Butter with Hemp Seed Butter!

Tahini (Sesame Seed Butter) Protein Bars
... swap the Sunflower Seed Butter with Roasted Tahini!

FRUITY FLAVORS

RASPBERRY ALMOND PROTEIN BARS

Yield: 10 Protein Bars

85g (⅓ cup) Roasted Almond Butter
1 cup Unsweetened Vanilla Almond Milk
2 tablespoons Beet Juice, from a can of beets
¾ teaspoon Vanilla Crème-Flavored Liquid Stevia Extract
¾ teaspoon Raspberry Flavor
¾ teaspoon Almond Extract
135g (1 cup, lightly packed) Vanilla Brown Rice Protein Powder
120g (1 cup) Oat Flour
⅛ teaspoon Salt
½ cup Freeze-Dried Raspberries, ground into a powder (measure after grinding)

Nutrition Facts	
Serving Size 1 Raspberry Almond Protein Bar (66g)	
Amount Per Serving	
Calories 170	Calories from Fat 50
	%Daily Value*
Total Fat 5.5g	8%
Saturated Fat .5g	2%
Trans Fat 0g	
Cholesterol 0mg	0%
Sodium 80mg	3%
Total Carbohydrate 15g	5%
Dietary Fiber 4g	19%
Sugars 2g	
Protein 13.5g	
Vitamin A 0% • Vitamin C 10%	
Calcium 10% • Iron 15%	

① Line an 8x8" brownie pan with parchment paper. Set aside.
② In an electric stand mixer bowl fitted with a beater attachment, add all of the ingredients. Mix on low speed until everything is fully incorporated. Feel free to sift the raspberry powder through a fine mesh sieve if you want to avoid the seeds.
③ Scrape down the sides of the bowl. Mix on medium speed for one last mix. Mixture should be thick and fudgy, like cookie dough.
④ Scoop the mixture into the brownie pan and flatten it out. Tightly cover the pan with plastic wrap and refrigerate overnight.
⑤ Lift the mixture out of the pan. Slice into 10 bars. Individually wrap the protein bars in plastic sandwich baggies and refrigerate to store (keeps for ~1 week).

ORANGE CRANBERRY PROTEIN BARS

Yield: 10 Protein Bars

85g (⅓ cup) Raw Almond Butter
1 cup + 2 tablespoons Unsweetened Vanilla Almond Milk
1 tablespoon Orange Zest
1 teaspoon Vanilla Crème-Flavored Liquid Stevia Extract
168g (1¼ cups, lightly packed) Vanilla Brown Rice Protein Powder
90g (¾ cup) Oat Flour
26g (¼ cup) Quinoa Flakes
⅛ teaspoon Salt
½ cup Dried Cranberries (no sugar added)

Nutrition Facts		
Serving Size 1 Orange Cranberry Protein Bar (72g)		
Amount Per Serving		
Calories 190	Calories from Fat 60	
		%Daily Value*
Total Fat 6g		**10%**
Saturated Fat 0.5g		**3%**
Trans Fat 0g		
Cholesterol 0mg		**0%**
Sodium 95mg		**4%**
Total Carbohydrate 18g		**6%**
Dietary Fiber 4g		**16%**
Sugars 6g		
Protein 16g		
Vitamin A 0%	•	Vitamin C 0%
Calcium 15%	•	Iron 15%

① Line an 8x8" brownie pan with parchment paper. Set aside.
② In an electric stand mixer bowl fitted with a beater attachment, add the almond butter, almond milk, orange zest and stevia extract. Mix on low speed while you prepare the dry ingredients.
③ In a medium-sized mixing bowl, whisk together the protein powder, oat flour, quinoa flakes and salt. Turn off the stand mixer and dump in the dry ingredients. Return mixer to low speed and mix until the dry ingredients are fully incorporated. Scrape down the sides of the bowl, add the chopped cranberries, then return to low speed for one last mix. Mixture should be thick and fudgy, like cookie dough.
④ Scoop the mixture into the brownie pan and flatten it out. Tightly cover the pan with plastic wrap and refrigerate overnight.
⑤ Lift the mixture out of the pan. Slice into 10 bars. Individually wrap the protein bars in plastic sandwich baggies and refrigerate to store (keeps for ~1 week).

CHOCOLATE-COVERED STRAWBERRY PROTEIN BARS

Yield: 12 Protein Bars

PROTEIN BARS

85g (⅓ cup) Roasted Almond Butter
1 cup Unsweetened Vanilla Almond Milk
2 tablespoons Beet Juice, from a can of beets
1 teaspoon Strawberry Flavor
¾ teaspoon Vanilla Crème-Flavored Liquid Stevia Extract
168g (1¼ cups, lightly packed) Vanilla Brown Rice Protein Powder
¾ cup Freeze-Dried Strawberries, ground into a powder (measure after grinding)
18g (2 tablespoons) Coconut Flour
⅛ teaspoon Salt

CHOCOLATE COATING

6oz Bittersweet Chocolate (70% cacao), melted

FOR THE PROTEIN BARS

① Line an 8x8" brownie pan with parchment paper. Set aside.
② In an electric stand mixer bowl fitted with a beater attachment, add the almond butter, almond milk, beet juice, strawberry flavor and stevia extract. Mix on low speed while you prepare the dry ingredients.
③ In a medium-sized mixing bowl, whisk together the protein powder, freeze-dried strawberry powder, coconut flour and salt. Turn off the stand mixer and dump in the dry ingredients. Return mixer to low speed and mix until the dry ingredients are fully incorporated. Scrape down the sides of the bowl if necessary. Mixture should be thick and fudgy, like cookie dough.
④ Scoop the mixture into the brownie pan and flatten it out. Tightly cover the pan with plastic wrap and refrigerate overnight.
⑤ Lift the mixture out of the pan. Slice into 12 bars.

FOR THE CHOCOLATE COATING

⑥ Place a silicone baking mat on top of a jelly roll pan and line the protein bars on top. With a large spoon, ladle the melted chocolate over the protein bars. Try to encase the entire protein bar with chocolate, but it doesn't have to be perfect.
⑦ Refrigerate until firm (~1 hour). Individually wrap the protein bars in plastic sandwich baggies and refrigerate to store (keeps for ~1 week).

Nutrition Facts

Serving Size 1 Chocolate-Covered
Strawberry Protein Bar (66g)

Amount Per Serving

Calories 190   Calories from Fat 80

%Daily Value*

Total Fat 9g	**14**%
Saturated Fat 4g	**20**%
Trans Fat 0g	
Cholesterol 0mg	**0**%
Sodium 75mg	**3**%
Total Carbohydrate 17g	**6**%
Dietary Fiber 5g	**21**%
Sugars 7g	
Protein 13g	

Vitamin A 0%	•	Vitamin C 35%
Calcium 10%	•	Iron 15%

CARAMEL APPLE PROTEIN BARS

Yield: 10 Protein Bars

PROTEIN BARS

262g (1 cup + 1 tablespoon) Unsweetened Applesauce
85g (⅓ cup) Roasted Cashew Butter
1 teaspoon Vanilla Crème-Flavored Liquid Stevia Extract
1 teaspoon Natural Butter Flavor
168g (1¼ cups, lightly packed) Vanilla Brown Rice Protein Powder
40g (⅓ cup) Oat Flour
34g (⅓ cup) Quinoa Flakes
1 tablespoon Ground Cinnamon
¼ teaspoon Salt

CARAMEL LAYER

105g (⅓ cup) Organic Caramel Sauce (see Pantry Staples on pg. ix)
75g (½ cup, packed) Vanilla Brown Rice Protein Powder

FOR THE PROTEIN BARS

① Line an 8x8" brownie pan with parchment paper. Set aside.
② In an electric stand mixer bowl fitted with a beater attachment, add all of the ingredients. Mix on low speed until everything is fully incorporated.
③ Scrape down the sides of the bowl. Mix on medium speed for one last mix. Mixture should be thick and fudgy, like cookie dough.
④ Scoop the mixture into the brownie pan and flatten it out.

FOR THE CARAMEL LAYER

⑤ In a small bowl, stir together the caramel sauce and protein powder. Mixture should be like a thick, slightly sticky frosting. Spoon the mixture over the protein bar base and spread to the edges of the pan (I used an offset spatula). Place in the freezer uncovered for 1 hour.
⑥ Lift the mixture out of the pan. Slice into 10 bars. To store, simply place a sheet of parchment paper on top of a cake pedestal, arrange the protein bars on top, and cover with a cake dome (keeps for 1 week).

Nutrition Facts	
Serving Size 1 Caramel Apple Protein Bar (79g)	
Amount Per Serving	
Calories 210	Calories from Fat 40
	%Daily Value*
Total Fat 4g	7%
Saturated Fat 0.5g	4%
Trans Fat 0g	
Cholesterol 0mg	0%
Sodium 130mg	5%
Total Carbohydrate 24g	8%
Dietary Fiber 4g	14%
Sugars 12g	
Protein 20g	
Vitamin A 0% • Vitamin C 6%	
Calcium 0% • Iron 15%	

Sweet, chewy, and rich ... it's hard to believe these
CARAMEL APPLE DIY PROTEIN BARS
are free of butter, cream, corn syrup and refined sugar!

CHERRY PIE PROTEIN BARS

Yield: 10 Protein Bars

85g (⅓ cup) Raw Almond Butter
1 cup Unsweetened Vanilla Almond Milk
1 teaspoon Cherry Flavor
¾ teaspoon Vanilla Crème-Flavored Liquid Stevia Extract
1⅓ cups Freeze-Dried Cherries, ground into a powder (measure after grinding)
168g (1¼ cups, lightly packed) Vanilla Brown Rice Protein Powder
30g (¼ cup) Oat Flour
¼ teaspoon Salt

① Line an 8x8" brownie pan with parchment paper. Set aside.
② In an electric stand mixer bowl fitted with a beater attachment, add all of the ingredients. Mix on low speed until everything is fully incorporated.
③ Scrape down the sides of the bowl. Mix on medium speed for one last mix. Mixture should be thick and fudgy, like cookie dough.
④ Scoop the mixture into the brownie pan and flatten it out. Tightly cover the pan with plastic wrap and refrigerate overnight.
⑤ Lift the mixture out of the pan. Slice into 10 bars. Individually wrap the protein bars in plastic sandwich baggies and refrigerate to store (keeps for ~1 week).

Nutrition Facts	
Serving Size 1 Cherry Pie Protein Bar (69g)	
Amount Per Serving	
Calories 190	Calories from Fat 45
	%Daily Value*
Total Fat 4.5g	**7%**
Saturated Fat 0g	**2%**
Trans Fat 0g	
Cholesterol 0mg	**0%**
Sodium 140mg	**6%**
Total Carbohydrate 20g	**7%**
Dietary Fiber 4g	**18%**
Sugars 12g	
Protein 16g	
Vitamin A 15% •	Vitamin C 4%
Calcium 10% •	Iron 15%

BANANA BREAD PROTEIN BARS

Yield: 10 Protein Bars

85g (⅓ cup) Roasted Walnut Butter
1 cup Unsweetened Vanilla Almond Milk
1 teaspoon Vanilla Crème-Flavored Liquid Stevia Extract
1 teaspoon Banana Flavor
1 teaspoon Natural Butter Flavor
168g (1¼ cups, lightly packed) Vanilla Brown Rice Protein Powder
3.5oz (1½ cups) Freeze-Dried Bananas
40g (⅓ cup) Oat Flour
1 tablespoon Ground Cinnamon
¼ teaspoon Salt

Nutrition Facts

Serving Size 1 Banana Bread Protein Bar (65g)

Amount Per Serving		
Calories 180		Calories from Fat 50
		%Daily Value*
Total Fat 6g		**9%**
Saturated Fat 0.5g		**3%**
Trans Fat 0g		
Cholesterol 0mg		**0%**
Sodium 120mg		**5%**
Total Carbohydrate 17g		**6%**
Dietary Fiber 4g		**15%**
Sugars 8g		
Protein 14g		
Vitamin A 0%	•	Vitamin C 0%
Calcium 6%	•	Iron 10%

① Line an 8x8" brownie pan with parchment paper. Set aside.
② In an electric stand mixer bowl fitted with a beater attachment, add all of the ingredients. Mix on low speed until everything is fully incorporated. Feel free to add ¼ cup of chopped walnuts!
③ Scrape down the sides of the bowl. Mix on medium speed for one last mix. Mixture should be thick and fudgy, like cookie dough, but with small chunks of banana throughout.
④ Scoop the mixture into the brownie pan and flatten it out. Tightly cover the pan with plastic wrap and refrigerate overnight.
⑤ Lift the mixture out of the pan. Slice into 10 bars. Individually wrap the protein bars in plastic sandwich baggies and refrigerate to store (keeps for ~1 week).

BLUEBERRY MUFFIN PROTEIN BARS

Yield: 10 Protein Bars

85g (⅓ cup) Roasted Walnut Butter
1 cup + 2 tablespoons Unsweetened Vanilla Almond Milk
1 teaspoon Lemon Zest
1 teaspoon Natural Butter Flavor
¾ teaspoon Vanilla Crème-Flavored Liquid Stevia Extract
¾ teaspoon Blueberry Flavor
168g (1¼ cups, lightly packed) Vanilla Brown Rice Protein Powder
80g (⅔ cup) Oat Flour
28g (¼ cup) Quick-Cooking Oats
¼ teaspoon Salt
¾ cup Dried Blueberries (no sugar added)

① Line an 8x8" brownie pan with parchment paper. Set aside.
② In an electric stand mixer bowl fitted with a beater attachment, add all of the ingredients. Mix on low speed until everything is fully incorporated. Feel free to add ¼ cup of chopped walnuts!
③ Scrape down the sides of the bowl. Mix on medium speed for one last mix. Mixture should be thick and fudgy, like cookie dough.
④ Scoop the mixture into the brownie pan and flatten it out. Tightly cover the pan with plastic wrap and refrigerate overnight.
⑤ Lift the mixture out of the pan. Slice into 10 bars. Individually wrap the protein bars in plastic sandwich baggies and refrigerate to store (keeps for ~1 week).

Nutrition Facts	
Serving Size 1 Blueberry Muffin Protein Bar (76g)	
Amount Per Serving	
Calories 200	Calories from Fat 60
	%Daily Value*
Total Fat 7g	**10%**
Saturated Fat 0.5g	**3%**
Trans Fat 0g	
Cholesterol 0mg	**0%**
Sodium 110mg	**5%**
Total Carbohydrate 20g	**7%**
Dietary Fiber 4g	**18%**
Sugars 5g	
Protein 16g	
Vitamin A 0%	Vitamin C 0%
Calcium 10%	Iron 15%

Sweet, chewy and fruity ... you'd never know these
BLUEBERRY MUFFIN DIY PROTEIN BARS
are free of butter, oil, and refined sugars!
Plus, they're gluten-free and vegan to boot!

"BAKED" FLAVORS

COOKIE DOUGH PROTEIN BARS

Yield: 10 Protein Bars

128g (½ cup) Roasted Almond Butter
1 cup + 2 tablespoons Unsweetened Vanilla Almond Milk
1 teaspoon Vanilla Crème-Flavored Liquid Stevia Extract
1 teaspoon Natural Butter Flavor
168g (1¼ cups, lightly packed) Vanilla Brown Rice Protein Powder
80g (⅔ cup) Oat Flour
¼ teaspoon Salt
¼ cup Mini Semi-Sweet Chocolate Chips

Nutrition Facts		
Serving Size 1 Chocolate Chip Cookie Dough Protein Bar (72g)		
Amount Per Serving		
Calories 200		Calories from Fat 80
		%Daily Value*
Total Fat 9g		**14%**
Saturated Fat 1.5g		**7%**
Trans Fat 0g		
Cholesterol 0mg		**0%**
Sodium 110mg		**5%**
Total Carbohydrate 14g		**5%**
Dietary Fiber 4g		**18%**
Sugars 4g		
Protein 17g		
Vitamin A 0%	•	Vitamin C 0%
Calcium 15%	•	Iron 15%

① Line an 8x8" brownie pan with parchment paper. Set aside.
② In an electric stand mixer bowl fitted with a beater attachment, add all of the ingredients. Mix on low speed until everything is fully incorporated.
③ Scrape down the sides of the bowl. Mix on medium speed for one last mix. Mixture should be thick and fudgy, like cookie dough (for *real*, this time!).
④ Scoop the mixture into the brownie pan and flatten it out. Tightly cover the pan with plastic wrap and refrigerate overnight.
⑤ Lift the mixture out of the pan. Slice into 10 bars. Individually wrap the protein bars in plastic sandwich baggies and refrigerate to store (keeps for ~1 week).

OATMEAL RAISIN PROTEIN COOKIES

Yield: 9 Protein Cookies

128g (½ cup) Roasted Walnut Butter
1 cup + 2 tablespoons Unsweetened Vanilla Almond Milk
1 teaspoon Vanilla Crème-Flavored Liquid Stevia Extract
½ teaspoon Natural Butter Flavor
168g (1¼ cups, lightly packed) Vanilla Brown Rice Protein Powder
80g (⅔ cup) Oat Flour
1½ teaspoons Ground Cinnamon
¼ teaspoon Salt
⅓ cup Raisins, chopped

Nutrition Facts

Serving Size 1 Oatmeal Raisin Cookie Protein Cookie (70g)

Amount Per Serving	
Calories 190	Calories from Fat 80

	%Daily Value*
Total Fat 9g	**14%**
Saturated Fat 1g	**5%**
Trans Fat 0g	
Cholesterol 0mg	**0%**
Sodium 120mg	**4%**
Total Carbohydrate 14g	**5%**
Dietary Fiber 4g	**16%**
Sugars 4g	
Protein 16g	

Vitamin A 2%	•	Vitamin C 0%
Calcium 10%	•	Iron 15%

① Line an 8x8" brownie pan (or 9x9" for thinner cookies) with parchment paper. Set aside.
② In an electric stand mixer bowl fitted with a beater attachment, add the walnut butter, almond milk, stevia extract and butter flavor. Mix on low speed while you prepare the dry ingredients.
③ In a medium-sized mixing bowl, whisk together the protein powder, oat flour, cinnamon and salt. Turn off the stand mixer and dump in the dry ingredients. Return mixer to low speed and mix until the dry ingredients are fully incorporated. Scrape down the sides of the bowl, add the raisins, then return to low speed for one last mix. Mixture should be thick and fudgy, like cookie dough.
④ Scoop the mixture into the brownie pan and flatten it out. Tightly cover the pan with plastic wrap and refrigerate overnight.
⑤ Lift the mixture out of the pan. Use a circle cookie cutter to punch out 9 cookies (use a 2½" cutter with an 8" pan and 2¾" cutter with a 9" pan). Wrap the protein cookies in plastic sandwich baggies and refrigerate to store (keeps for ~1 week). The remaining protein bar dough leftover after punching out the cookies can be snacked on (by the cook, of course!) or reshaped into a cookie or bar.

WHITE CHOCOLATE MACADAMIA PROTEIN COOKIES

Yield: 9 Protein Cookies

PROTEIN COOKIES

128g (½ cup) Roasted Macadamia Butter
1 cup + 2 tablespoons Unsweetened Vanilla Almond Milk
1 teaspoon Vanilla Crème-Flavored Liquid Stevia Extract
½ teaspoon Natural Butter Flavor
168g (1¼ cups, lightly packed) Vanilla Brown Rice Protein Powder
80g (⅔ cup) Oat Flour
¼ teaspoon Salt

WHITE CHOCOLATE COATING

6oz White Chocolate, melted

FOR THE PROTEIN COOKIES

① Line an 8x8" brownie pan (or 9x9" for thinner cookies) with parchment paper. Set aside.
② In an electric stand mixer bowl fitted with a beater attachment, add the macadamia butter, almond milk, stevia extract and butter flavor. Mix on low speed while you prepare the dry ingredients.
③ In a medium-sized mixing bowl, whisk together the protein powder, oat flour and salt. Turn off the stand mixer and dump in the dry ingredients. Return mixer to low speed and mix until the dry ingredients are fully incorporated. Scrape down the sides of the bowl if necessary. Mixture should be thick and fudgy, like cookie dough.
④ Scoop the mixture into the brownie pan and flatten it out. Tightly cover the pan with plastic wrap and refrigerate overnight.
⑤ Lift the mixture out of the pan. Use a circle cookie cutter to punch out 9 cookies (use a 2½" cutter with an 8" pan, or 2¾" cutter with a 9" pan). The remaining protein bar dough leftover after punching out the cookies can be snacked on or reshaped into a cookie or bar.

FOR THE WHITE CHOCOLATE COATING

⑥ Place a silicone baking mat on top of a jelly roll pan and line the protein cookies on top. Place a protein cookie on the prongs of a large fork and dunk into the melted white chocolate. With a large spoon, ladle the chocolate over the cookie. Gently slide the cookie onto the silicone baking mat. Repeat this process with the rest of the protein cookies.
⑦ Refrigerate until firm (·2 hours). Individually wrap the protein cookies in plastic sandwich baggies and refrigerate to store (keeps for ~1 week).

Nutrition Facts

Serving Size 1 White Chocolate
Macadamia Cookie Protein Cookie (82g)

Amount Per Serving

Calories 290	Calories from Fat 150

	%Daily Value*
Total Fat 16.5g	**25**%
Saturated Fat 5g	**25**%
Trans Fat 0g	
Cholesterol < 5mg	**1**%
Sodium 140mg	**4**%
Total Carbohydrate 20g	**7**%
Dietary Fiber 4g	**14**%
Sugars 10g	
Protein 16g	

Vitamin A 0%	•	Vitamin C 0%
Calcium 15%	•	Iron 10%

FUN PROTEIN FACT

Athletes need more protein because regular exercise causes tissue damage, which stimulates tissue growth!

RED VELVET CAKE PROTEIN BARS

Yield: 10 Protein Bars

PROTEIN BARS

165g (⅔ cup) Roasted Beet Puree (see Instructions below)
128g (½ cup) Raw Almond Butter
½ cup + 1 tablespoon Unsweetened Vanilla Almond Milk
1 tablespoon Natural Butter Flavor
1½ teaspoons Vanilla Crème-Flavored Liquid Stevia Extract
210g (1⅔ cups, lightly packed) Chocolate Brown Rice Protein Powder
80g (⅔ cup) Oat Flour
¼ teaspoon Salt

CHOCOLATE COATING

6oz Bittersweet Chocolate (70% cacao), melted

FOR THE ROASTED BEET PUREE

① Preheat your oven to 350 degrees Fahrenheit. Rinse and gently scrub two fist-sized beets, then wrap them completely in foil. Place the beets in a 9x9" brownie pan and bake for ~1½ hours, or until a fork pierces through the beets with ease
② Remove the beets from the oven, carefully unwrap the foil and let sit until it's cool enough to handle. Use a knife to scrape off the beet skins (they will fall off easily).
③ Chop the beets into chunks and place in a food processor. Puree until completely smooth.

FOR THE PROTEIN BARS

④ Line an 8x8" brownie pan with parchment paper. Set aside.
⑤ In an electric stand mixer bowl fitted with a beater attachment, add the beet puree, almond butter, almond milk, butter flavor and stevia extract. Mix on low speed while you prepare the dry ingredients.
⑥ In a medium-sized mixing bowl, whisk together the protein powder, oat flour and salt. Turn off the stand mixer and dump in the dry ingredients. Return mixer to low speed and mix until the dry ingredients are fully incorporated. Scrape down the sides of the bowl if necessary. Mixture should be thick and fudgy, like cookie dough.
⑦ Scoop the mixture into the brownie pan and flatten it out. Tightly cover the pan with plastic wrap and refrigerate overnight.
⑧ Lift the mixture out of the pan. Slice into 10 bars.

FOR THE CHOCOLATE COATING

⑨ Place a silicone baking mat on top of a jelly roll pan and line the protein bars on top. With a large spoon, ladle the melted chocolate over the protein bars. Try to encase the entire protein bar with chocolate, but it doesn't have to be perfect.

⑩ Refrigerate until firm (~1 hour). Individually wrap the protein bars in plastic sandwich baggies and refrigerate to store (keeps for ~1 week).

NOTE

Using canned or prepackaged cooked beets will not provide the same vibrant red color as using freshly roasted beets... the bars will turn out brown (yes, I tried it). For best results, use freshly roasted beet puree!

RED VELVET.
CAKE.
DIY PROTEIN BARS.
Need I say more?

Nutrition Facts	
Serving Size 1 Red Velvet Cake Protein Bar (91g)	

Amount Per Serving	
Calories 280	Calories from Fat 120
	%Daily Value*
Total Fat 14g	**21**%
Saturated Fat 4.5g	**23**%
Trans Fat 0g	
Cholesterol 0mg	**0**%
Sodium 110mg	**5**%
Total Carbohydrate 23g	**8**%
Dietary Fiber 6g	**24**%
Sugars 8g	
Protein 22g	
Vitamin A 2% •	Vitamin C 0%
Calcium 15% •	Iron 25%

CINNAMON ROLL PROTEIN SQUARES

Yield: 9 Protein Squares

PROTEIN SQUARES

128g (½ cup) Roasted Almond Butter
1 cup Unsweetened Vanilla Almond Milk
63g (3 tablespoons) Pure Maple Syrup
¾ teaspoon Vanilla Crème-Flavored Liquid Stevia Extract
½ teaspoon Natural Butter Flavor
168g (1¼ cups, lightly packed) Vanilla Brown Rice Protein Powder
90g (¾ cup) Oat Flour
2 teaspoons Ground Cinnamon
¼ teaspoon Salt

CREAM CHEESE FROSTING

4oz Neufchâtel Cream Cheese, room temperature (or ⅓ Less Fat Cream Cheese)
2 tablespoons Unsweetened Vanilla Almond Milk
¼ teaspoon Vanilla Crème-Flavored Liquid Stevia Extract
¼ teaspoon Natural Butter Flavor
⅛ teaspoon Vanilla Bean Paste

FOR THE PROTEIN SQUARES

① Line an 8x8" brownie pan with parchment paper. Set aside.
② In an electric stand mixer bowl fitted with a beater attachment, add all of the ingredients. Mix on low speed until everything is fully incorporated.
③ Scrape down the sides of the bowl. Mix on medium speed for one last mix. Mixture should be thick and fudgy, like cookie dough.
④ Scoop the mixture into the brownie pan and flatten it out. Tightly cover the pan with plastic wrap and refrigerate overnight.
⑤ Lift the mixture out of the pan. Slice into 9 squares.

Nutrition Facts	
Serving Size 1 Cinnamon Roll Protein Square (94g)	
Amount Per Serving	
Calories 240	Calories from Fat 100
	%Daily Value*
Total Fat 11g	17%
Saturated Fat 2.5g	12%
Trans Fat 0g	
Cholesterol 10mg	3%
Sodium 180mg	8%
Total Carbohydrate 18g	6%
Dietary Fiber 4g	17%
Sugars 6g	
Protein 19g	
Vitamin A 2% •	Vitamin C 0%
Calcium 10% •	Iron 15%

FOR THE CREAM CHEESE FROSTING

⑥ In a medium-sized mixing bowl, whisk together the cream cheese, almond milk, stevia extract, butter flavor and vanilla paste. Spread the frosting over the squares. To store, simply place a sheet of parchment paper on top of a cake pedestal, arrange the protein squares on top, and cover with a cake dome (keeps for ~1 week).

GERMAN CHOCOLATE CAKE PROTEIN BARS

Yield: 10 Protein Bars

PROTEIN BARS

128g (½ cup) Roasted Pecan Butter
1 cup + 2 tablespoons Unsweetened Vanilla Almond Milk
1 teaspoon Vanilla Crème-Flavored Liquid Stevia Extract
168g (1 ¼ cups, lightly packed) Chocolate Brown Rice Protein Powder
80g (⅔ cup) Oat Flour
¼ teaspoon Espresso Powder
¼ teaspoon Salt

TOPPINGS

2oz Bittersweet Chocolate (70% cacao), melted
2 tablespoons Reduced Fat Unsweetened Shredded Coconut
2 tablespoons Roasted Pecans, chopped

FOR THE PROTEIN BARS

① Line an 8x8" brownie pan with parchment paper. Set aside.
② In an electric stand mixer bowl fitted with a beater attachment, add the pecan butter, almond milk and stevia extract. Mix on low speed while you prepare the dry ingredients.
③ In a medium-sized mixing bowl, whisk together the protein powder, oat flour, espresso powder and salt. Turn off the stand mixer and dump in the dry ingredients. Return mixer to low speed and mix until the dry ingredients are fully incorporated. Scrape down the sides of the bowl if necessary. Mixture should be thick and fudgy, like cookie dough.
④ Scoop the mixture into the brownie pan and flatten it out. Tightly cover the pan with plastic wrap and refrigerate overnight.
⑤ Lift the mixture out of the pan. Slice into 10 bars.

FOR THE TOPPINGS

⑥ Place a silicone baking mat on top of a jelly roll pan and line the protein bars on top. Spread the melted chocolate over the protein bars, sprinkle with the shredded coconut, and press the chopped pecans on top.
⑦ Refrigerate until firm (1 hour). Individually wrap the protein bars in plastic sandwich baggies and refrigerate to store (keeps for ~1 week).

Nutrition Facts	
Serving Size 1 German Chocolate Cake Protein Bar (96g)	
Amount Per Serving	
Calories 220	Calories from Fat 120
	%Daily Value*
Total Fat 13g	**20%**
Saturated Fat 3g	**14%**
Trans Fat 0g	
Cholesterol 0mg	**0%**
Sodium 110mg	**3%**
Total Carbohydrate 11g	**4%**
Dietary Fiber 5g	**19%**
Sugars 3g	
Protein 16g	
Vitamin A 0% • Vitamin C 0%	
Calcium 10% • Iron 20%	

GERMAN CHOCOLATE CAKE is a chocolate layer cake with a caramel-coconut-pecan filling and topping. It's a super sweet, rich, decadent, and *heavy* cake. I'm sure you guessed it – it's packed with cups and cups of sugar, a little too many sticks of butter, and *thousands* of calories *PER* slice… Quite the opposite of these protein bars!

These (healthified) **GERMAN CHOCOLATE CAKE DIY PROTEIN BARS** are full of healthy fats, complex carbohydrates, a kick of fiber and a punch of protein. These surely won't weigh you down!

BIRTHDAY CAKE PROTEIN BARS

Yield: 12 Protein Bars

PROTEIN BARS

128g (½ cup) Raw Almond Butter
1 cup + 2 tablespoons Unsweetened Vanilla Almond Milk
2 teaspoons Natural Butter Flavor
1 teaspoon Vanilla Crème-Flavored Liquid Stevia Extract
¾ teaspoon Almond Extract
168g (1¼ cups, lightly packed) Vanilla Brown Rice Protein Powder
120g (1 cup) Oat Flour
¼ teaspoon Salt

CREAM CHEESE FROSTING

4oz Neufchâtel Cream Cheese, room temperature (or ⅓ Less Fat Cream Cheese)
2 tablespoons Unsweetened Vanilla Almond Milk
½ teaspoon Vanilla Crème-Flavored Liquid Stevia Extract
¼ cup Natural Rainbow Sprinkles

FOR THE PROTEIN BARS

① Line an 8x8" brownie pan with parchment paper. Set aside.
② In an electric stand mixer bowl fitted with a beater attachment, add all of the ingredients. Mix on low speed until everything is fully incorporated.
③ Scrape down the sides of the bowl. Mix on medium speed for one last mix. Mixture should be thick and fudgy, like cookie dough.
④ Scoop the mixture into the brownie pan and flatten it out.

FOR THE CREAM CHEESE FROSTING

⑤ In a medium-sized mixing bowl, whisk together the cream cheese, almond milk and stevia extract. Scoop mixture over the protein bar base and spread to the edges of the pan (I used an offset spatula). Place in the freezer uncovered for 1 hour.
⑥ Lift the mixture out of the pan. Slice into 12 bars.
⑦ Scatter the sprinkles on top. To store, simply place a sheet of parchment paper on top of a cake pedestal, arrange the protein bars on top, and cover with a cake dome (keeps for ~1 week).

Nutrition Facts	
Serving Size 1 Birthday Cake Protein Bar (74g)	
Amount Per Serving	
Calories 200	Calories from Fat 80
	%Daily Value*
Total Fat 8g	13%
Saturated Fat 2g	9%
Trans Fat 0g	
Cholesterol 5mg	2%
Sodium 140mg	6%
Total Carbohydrate 18g	5%
Dietary Fiber 3g	14%
Sugars 4g	
Protein 15g	
Vitamin A 0%	Vitamin C 0%
Calcium 8%	Iron 10%

CARROT CAKE PROTEIN BARS

Yield: 10 Protein Bars

128g (½ cup) Roasted Walnut Butter
1 cup + 2 tablespoons Unsweetened Vanilla Almond Milk
¾ teaspoon Vanilla Crème-Flavored Liquid Stevia Extract
168g (1¼ cups, lightly packed) Vanilla Brown Rice Protein Powder
90g (¾ cup) Oat Flour
1¾ teaspoons Ground Cinnamon
¼ teaspoon Ground Nutmeg
¼ teaspoon Salt
1-1½ cups Grated Carrots
¼-½ cup Reduced Fat Unsweetened Shredded Coconut
¼ cup Raisins, chopped

Nutrition Facts	
Serving Size 1 Carrot Cake Protein Bar (86g)	
Amount Per Serving	
Calories 210	Calories from Fat 90
	%Daily Value*
Total Fat 10g	15%
Saturated Fat 1.5g	6%
Trans Fat 0g	
Cholesterol 0mg	0%
Sodium 120mg	5%
Total Carbohydrate 15g	5%
Dietary Fiber 4g	17%
Sugars 4g	
Protein 16g	
Vitamin A 55% • Vitamin C 0%	
Calcium 10% • Iron 15%	

① Line an 8x8" brownie pan with parchment paper. Set aside.
② In an electric stand mixer bowl fitted with a beater attachment, add the walnut butter, almond milk and stevia extract. Mix on low speed while you prepare the dry ingredients.
③ In a medium-sized mixing bowl, whisk together the protein powder, oat flour, cinnamon, nutmeg and salt. Turn off the stand mixer and dump in the dry ingredients. Return mixer to low speed and mix until the ingredients are fully incorporated. Scrape down the sides of the bowl, add the grated carrots, shredded coconut and raisins, then return to low speed for one last mix. Mixture should be thick and fudgy, like cookie dough.
④ Scoop the mixture into the brownie pan and flatten it out. Tightly cover the pan with plastic wrap and refrigerate overnight.
⑤ Lift the mixture out of the pan. Slice into 10 bars. Individually wrap the protein bars in plastic sandwich baggies and refrigerate to store (keeps for ~1 week). If you're craving a little more decadent, consider topping these with Cream Cheese Frosting (pg. 29)!

SEVEN SINS PROTEIN BARS

(like a Seven Layer Bar transformed into a protein bar!)

Yield: 12 Protein Bars

128g (½ cup) Roasted Pecan Butter
1 cup Unsweetened Vanilla Almond Milk
1 teaspoon Natural Butterscotch Flavor
½ teaspoon English Toffee-Flavored Liquid Stevia Extract
168g (1¼ cups, lightly packed) Vanilla Brown Rice Protein Powder
80g (⅔ cup) Oat Flour
½ cup Reduced Fat Unsweetened Shredded Coconut
½ cup Mini Semi-Sweet Chocolate Chips
½ cup Graham Cracker Crumbs
¼ teaspoon Salt

Nutrition Facts	
Serving Size 1 Seven Sins Protein Bar (67g)	

Amount Per Serving	
Calories 220	Calories from Fat 110
	%Daily Value*
Total Fat 12g	**19%**
Saturated Fat 3g	**15%**
Trans Fat 0g	
Cholesterol 0mg	**0%**
Sodium 130mg	**6%**
Total Carbohydrate 16g	**5%**
Dietary Fiber 4g	**17%**
Sugars 6g	
Protein 13g	
Vitamin A 0% • Vitamin C 0%	
Calcium 6% • Iron 15%	

① Line an 8x8" brownie pan with parchment paper. Set aside.
② In an electric stand mixer bowl fitted with a beater attachment, add all of the ingredients. Mix on low speed until everything is fully incorporated.
③ Scrape down the sides of the bowl. Mix on medium speed for one last mix. Mixture should be thick and fudgy, like cookie dough.
④ Scoop the mixture into the brownie pan and flatten it out. Tightly cover the pan with plastic wrap and refrigerate overnight.
⑤ Lift the mixture out of the pan. Slice into 12 bars. Individually wrap the protein bars in plastic sandwich baggies and refrigerate to store (keeps for ~1 week).

PUMPKIN PIE PROTEIN BARS

Yield: 12 Protein Bars

one 15oz can 100% Pure Pumpkin Puree
128g (½ cup) Roasted Almond Butter
¾ teaspoon English Toffee-Flavored Liquid Stevia Extract
1½ cups Graham Cracker Crumbs
168g (1¼ cups, lightly packed) Vanilla Brown Rice Protein Powder
30g (¼ cup) Oat Flour
1 tablespoon Ground Cinnamon (or a mix of Ground Cinnamon + Pumpkin Pie Spice)
⅛ teaspoon Salt

① Line an 8x8" brownie pan with parchment paper. Set aside.
② In an electric stand mixer bowl fitted with a beater attachment, add all of the ingredients. Mix on low speed until everything is fully incorporated.
③ Scrape down the sides of the bowl. Mix on medium speed for one last mix. Mixture should be thick and fudgy, like cookie dough.
④ Scoop the mixture into the brownie pan and flatten it out. Tightly cover the pan with plastic wrap and refrigerate overnight.
⑤ Lift the mixture out of the pan. Slice into 12 bars. Individually wrap the protein bars in plastic sandwich baggies and refrigerate to store (keeps for ~1 week).

Nutrition Facts	
Serving Size 1 Pumpkin Pie Protein Bar (80g)	
Amount Per Serving	
Calories 200	Calories from Fat 60
	%Daily Value*
Total Fat 7g	**11%**
Saturated Fat 0g	**1%**
Trans Fat 0g	
Cholesterol 0mg	**0%**
Sodium 160mg	**7%**
Total Carbohydrate 20g	**7%**
Dietary Fiber 5g	**22%**
Sugars 4.5g	
Protein 14g	
Vitamin A 110% • Vitamin C 2%	
Calcium 6% • Iron 15%	

PECAN PIE PROTEIN BARS

Yield: 12 Protein Bars

128g (½ cup) Roasted Pecan Butter
1 cup Unsweetened Vanilla Almond Milk
1 teaspoon English Toffee-Flavored Liquid Stevia Extract
1½ cups Graham Cracker Crumbs
168g (1¼ cups, lightly packed) Vanilla Brown Rice Protein Powder
40g (⅓ cup) Oat Flour
1½ teaspoons Ground Cinnamon
¼ teaspoon Salt

Nutrition Facts

Serving Size 1 Pecan Pie Protein Bar (65g)

Amount Per Serving	
Calories 200	Calories from Fat 90

	%Daily Value*
Total Fat 9.5g	**15%**
Saturated Fat 0.5g	**4%**
Trans Fat 0g	
Cholesterol 0mg	**0%**
Sodium 200mg	**8%**
Total Carbohydrate 16.5g	**5%**
Dietary Fiber 4g	**17%**
Sugars 4g	
Protein 13g	

Vitamin A 0%	•	Vitamin C 0%
Calcium 8%	•	Iron 10%

① Line an 8x8" brownie pan with parchment paper. Set aside.
② In an electric stand mixer bowl fitted with a beater attachment, add all of the ingredients. Mix on low speed until everything is fully incorporated.
③ Scrape down the sides of the bowl. Mix on medium speed for one last mix. Mixture should be thick and fudgy, like cookie dough.
④ Scoop the mixture into the brownie pan and flatten it out. Tightly cover the pan with plastic wrap and refrigerate overnight.
⑤ Lift the mixture out of the pan. Slice into 12 bars. Individually wrap the protein bars in plastic sandwich baggies and refrigerate to store (keeps for ~1 week).

TIRAMISÙ PROTEIN BARS

Yield: 12 Protein Bars

PROTEIN BARS

128g (½ cup) Raw Almond Butter
¾ cup Unsweetened Vanilla Almond Milk
¼ cup Brewed Espresso, cooled to room temperature
1 teaspoon Vanilla Crème-Flavored Liquid Stevia Extract
168g (1¼ cups, lightly packed) Vanilla Brown Rice Protein Powder
80g (⅔ cup) Oat Flour
½ teaspoon Espresso Powder
¼ teaspoon Salt

MASCARPONE FROSTING

4oz Mascarpone, room temperature
½ tablespoon Unsweetened Vanilla Almond Milk or Rum*
¼ teaspoon Vanilla Crème-Flavored Liquid Stevia Extract
2 tablespoons Unsweetened Dutch Processed Cocoa Powder

FOR THE PROTEIN BARS

① Line an 8x8" brownie pan with parchment paper. Set aside.
② In an electric stand mixer bowl fitted with a beater attachment, add all of the ingredients. Mix on low speed until everything is fully incorporated.
③ Scrape down the sides of the bowl. Mix on medium speed for one last mix. Mixture should be thick and fudgy, like cookie dough.
④ Scoop the mixture into the brownie pan and flatten it out.

FOR THE MASCARPONE FROSTING

⑤ In a medium-sized mixing bowl, whisk together the mascarpone, almond milk (or rum) and stevia extract. Scoop mixture over the protein bar base and spread to the edges of the pan (I used an offset spatula). Place in the freezer uncovered for 1 hour.
⑥ Lift the mixture out of the pan. Slice into 12 bars.
⑦ Lightly dust the cocoa powder over the bars. To store, simply place a sheet of parchment paper on top of a cake pedestal, arrange the protein bars on top, and cover with a cake dome (keeps for ~5 days).

Nutrition Facts	
Serving Size 1 Tiramisù Protein Bar (62g)	
Amount Per Serving	
Calories 190	Calories from Fat 90
	%Daily Value*
Total Fat 10g	**16%**
Saturated Fat 3.5g	**18%**
Trans Fat 0g	
Cholesterol 10mg	**3%**
Sodium 100mg	**4%**
Total Carbohydrate 9g	**3%**
Dietary Fiber 3g	**13%**
Sugars 1g	
Protein 14g	
Vitamin A 0% • Vitamin C 0%	
Calcium 8% • Iron 10%	

*If you're making these protein bars for *breakfast* and *snacks*, I would recommend using almond milk in the frosting. If you're making these protein bars for *dessert*, on other hand, I would recommend taking the "traditional" route and using rum instead!

"FANCY PANTS" FLAVORS

S'MORES PROTEIN BARS

Yield: 12 Protein Bars

PROTEIN BARS

128g (½ cup) Roasted Almond Butter
1 cup Unsweetened Vanilla Almond Milk
½ teaspoon Vanilla Crème-Flavored Liquid Stevia Extract
1⅓ cups Graham Cracker Crumbs
168g (1¼ cups, lightly packed) Chocolate Brown Rice Protein Powder
⅛ teaspoon Salt

TOPPINGS

6oz Bittersweet Chocolate (70% cacao), melted
120 (~1½ cups/5oz) All-Natural Mini Vanilla Marshmallows

FOR THE PROTEIN BARS

① Line an 8x8" brownie pan with parchment paper. Set aside.
② In electric stand mixer bowl fitted with a beater attachment, add the almond butter, almond milk and stevia extract. Mix on low speed while you prepare the dry ingredients.
③ In a medium-sized mixing bowl, whisk together the protein powder, graham cracker crumbs and salt. Turn off the stand mixer and dump in the dry ingredients. Return mixer to low speed and mix until the ingredients are fully incorporated. Scrape down the sides of the bowl if necessary. Mixture should be thick and fudgy, like cookie dough.
④ Scoop the mixture into the brownie pan and flatten it out. Tightly cover the pan with plastic wrap and refrigerate overnight.
⑤ Lift the mixture out of the pan. Slice into 12 bars.

FOR THE TOPPINGS

⑥ Place a silicone baking mat on top of a jelly roll pan and line the protein bars on top. With a large spoon, ladle the melted chocolate over the protein bars. Try to encase the entire protein bar with chocolate.
⑦ Press 10 mini marshmallows on top of each protein bar so they adhere as the chocolate firms up.
⑧ Refrigerate until firm (~1 hour). Individually wrap the protein bars in plastic sandwich baggies and refrigerate to store (keeps for ~5 days).

Nutrition Facts	
Serving Size 1 S'mores Protein Bar (85g)	
Amount Per Serving	
Calories 270	Calories from Fat 110
	%Daily Value*
Total Fat 12.5g	19%
Saturated Fat 4g	21%
Trans Fat 0g	
Cholesterol 0mg	0%
Sodium 160mg	7%
Total Carbohydrate 28g	9%
Dietary Fiber 5g	22%
Sugars 16g	
Protein 15g	
Vitamin A 0%	Vitamin C 0%
Calcium 10%	Iron 25%

Who needs a campfire when you've got these
S'MORES DIY PROTEIN BARS?
Seriously now.

MO-TELLA PROTEIN BARS

Yield: 10 Protein Bars

128g (½ cup) Roasted Hazelnut Butter
1 cup + 2 tablespoons Unsweetened Vanilla Almond Milk
1 teaspoon Vanilla Crème-Flavored Liquid Stevia Extract
168g (1¼ cups, lightly packed) Chocolate Brown Rice Protein Powder
60g (½ cup) Oat Flour
3 tablespoons Unsweetened Dutch Processed Cocoa Powder
¼ teaspoon Salt

Nutrition Facts	
Serving Size 1 Nutella® Protein Bar (65g)	
Amount Per Serving	
Calories 170	Calories from Fat 80
	%Daily Value*
Total Fat 9g	**13%**
Saturated Fat 1g	**4%**
Trans Fat 0g	
Cholesterol 0mg	**0%**
Sodium 110mg	**5%**
Total Carbohydrate 9g	**3%**
Dietary Fiber 4g	**16%**
Sugars 1g	
Protein 16g	
Vitamin A 0% •	Vitamin C 0%
Calcium 15% •	Iron 20%

① Line an 8x8" brownie pan with parchment paper. Set aside.
② In an electric stand mixer bowl fitted with a beater attachment, add all of the ingredients. Mix on low speed until everything is fully incorporated. Feel free to add ¼ cup of mini semi-sweet chocolate chips!
③ Scrape down the sides of the bowl. Mix on medium speed for one last mix. Mixture should be thick and fudgy, like cookie dough.
④ Scoop the mixture into the brownie pan and flatten it out. Tightly cover the pan with plastic wrap and refrigerate overnight.
⑤ Lift the mixture out of the pan. Slice into 10 bars. Individually wrap the protein bars in plastic sandwich baggies and refrigerate to store (keeps for ~1 week).

What are **MO-TELLA DIY PROTEIN BARS** you ask? They taste like they're made with Nutella®, except they're healthy, wholesome, and all natural. One bite and you'll be screaming, "Gimme mo of those **MO-TELLA PROTEIN BARS!**"

Nutella® is a registered trademark of Ferro, SpA. Ferro, SpA is not related in any way to Desserts with Benefits, Inc.

MOCHA PROTEIN BARS

Yield: 10 Protein Bars

128g (½ cup) Roasted Almond Butter
⅔ cup Unsweetened Vanilla Almond Milk
½ cup Brewed Espresso, cooled to room temperature
1 teaspoon Vanilla Crème-Flavored Liquid Stevia Extract
168g (1¼ cups, lightly packed) Chocolate Brown Rice Protein Powder
80g (⅔ cup) Oat Flour
2 tablespoons Unsweetened Natural Cocoa Powder
⅛ teaspoon Salt

① Line an 8x8" brownie pan with parchment paper. Set aside.
② In an electric stand mixer bowl fitted with a beater attachment, add all of the ingredients. Mix on low speed until everything is fully incorporated. Feel free to add ¼ cup of mini semi-sweet chocolate chips!
③ Scrape down the sides of the bowl. Mix on medium speed for one last mix. Mixture should be thick and fudgy, like cookie dough.
④ Scoop the mixture into the brownie pan and flatten it out. Tightly cover the pan with plastic wrap and refrigerate overnight.
⑤ Lift the mixture out of the pan. Slice into 10 bars. Individually wrap the protein bars in plastic sandwich baggies and refrigerate to store (keeps for ~1 week).

Nutrition Facts	
Serving Size 1 Mocha Protein Bar (67g)	
Amount Per Serving	
Calories 170	Calories from Fat 70
	%Daily Value*
Total Fat 7g	**11%**
Saturated Fat 0.5g	**3%**
Trans Fat 0g	
Cholesterol 0mg	**0%**
Sodium 75mg	**3%**
Total Carbohydrate 10g	**3%**
Dietary Fiber 4g	**16%**
Sugars 1g	
Protein 17g	
Vitamin A 8%	Vitamin C 0%
Calcium 10%	Iron 15%

CARAMEL MACCHIATO PROTEIN BARS

Yield: 12 Protein Bars

PROTEIN BARS

128g (½ cup) Roasted Cashew Butter
⅔ cup Unsweetened Vanilla Almond Milk
½ cup Brewed Espresso, cooled to room temperature
1 teaspoon Vanilla Bean Paste
1 teaspoon English Toffee-Flavored Liquid Stevia Extract
168g (1¼ cups, lightly packed) Vanilla Brown Rice Protein Powder
120g (1 cup) Oat Flour
¼ teaspoon Salt

CARAMEL-COFFEE FROSTING

105g (⅓ cup) Organic Caramel Sauce (see Pantry Staples on pg. ix)
75g (½ cup, packed) Vanilla Brown Rice Protein Powder
½ teaspoon Espresso Powder

FOR THE PROTEIN BARS

① Line an 8x8" brownie pan with parchment paper. Set aside.
② In an electric stand mixer bowl fitted with a beater attachment, add all of the ingredients. Mix on low speed until everything is fully incorporated.
③ Scrape down the sides of the bowl. Mix on medium speed for one last mix. Mixture should be thick and fudgy, like cookie dough.
④ Scoop the mixture into the brownie pan and flatten it out.

FOR THE CARAMEL-COFFEE FROSTING

⑤ In a small bowl, whisk together the caramel sauce, protein powder and espresso powder. Mixture should be like a thick, slightly sticky frosting. Spoon the mixture over the protein bar base and spread to the edges of the pan (I used an offset spatula). Place in the freezer uncovered for 1 hour.
⑥ Lift the mixture out of the pan. Slice into 12 bars. To store, simply place a sheet of parchment paper on top of a cake pedestal, arrange the protein bars on top, and cover with a cake dome (keeps for ~1 week).

Nutrition Facts	
Serving Size 1 Caramel Macchiato Protein Bar (74g)	
Amount Per Serving	
Calories 200	Calories from Fat 50
	%Daily Value*
Total Fat 5.5g	9%
Saturated Fat 1g	5%
Trans Fat 0g	
Cholesterol 0mg	0%
Sodium 115mg	5%
Total Carbohydrate 21g	7%
Dietary Fiber 3g	13%
Sugars 8g	
Protein 18g	
Vitamin A 0%	Vitamin C 0%
Calcium 4%	Iron 10%

Rich, fudgy, and satisfyingly sweet. And caffeinated too!
These **CARAMEL MACCHIATO DIY PROTEIN BARS**
are like dessert and coffee in one.
Pretty much the best of both worlds, am I right?
(Yes, I'm right. Don't argue with me.)

MINT CHOCOLATE PROTEIN BARS

Yield: 12 Protein Bars

PROTEIN BARS

1 cup + 2 tablespoons Unsweetened Vanilla Almond Milk
3 cups Baby Spinach, packed
128g (½ cup) Raw Almond Butter
2 teaspoons Vanilla Crème-Flavored Liquid Stevia Extract
2 teaspoons Mint Flavor
168g (1¼ cups, lightly packed) Vanilla Brown Rice Protein Powder
120g (1 cup) Oat Flour
1½ tablespoons Psyllium Husk Powder
⅛ teaspoon Salt

CHOCOLATE COATING

6oz Bittersweet Chocolate (70% cacao), melted
2 teaspoons Mint Flavor

FOR THE PROTEIN BARS

① Line an 8x8" brownie pan with parchment paper. Set aside.
② In a food processor, blend together the almond milk and spinach until completely smooth.
③ In an electric stand mixer bowl fitted with a beater attachment, add the "green milk" mixture, almond butter, stevia extract and mint flavor. Mix on low speed while you prepare the dry ingredients.
④ In a medium-sized mixing bowl, whisk together the protein powder, oat flour, psyllium husk powder and salt. Turn off the stand mixer and dump in the dry ingredients. Return mixer to low speed and mix until the dry ingredients are fully incorporated. Scrape down the sides of the bowl if necessary. Mixture should be thick and fudgy, like cookie dough.
⑤ Scoop the mixture into the brownie pan and flatten it out. Tightly cover the pan with plastic wrap and refrigerate overnight.
⑥ Lift the mixture out of the pan. Slice into 12 bars.

FOR THE CHOCOLATE COATING

⑦ Stir the mint flavor into the melted chocolate.
⑧ Place a silicone baking mat on top of a jelly roll pan and line the protein bars on top. With a large spoon, ladle the melted chocolate over the protein bars. Try to encase the entire protein bar with chocolate, but it doesn't have to be perfect.
⑨ Refrigerate until firm (~1 hour). Individually wrap the protein bars in plastic sandwich baggies and refrigerate to store (keeps for ~4 days).

Sweet, chocolatey, and minty fresh – these
MINT CHOCOLATE DIY PROTEIN BARS
will be sure to brighten up your day!

Nutrition Facts		
Serving Size 1 Mint Chocolate Protein Bar (84g)		
Amount Per Serving		
Calories 240	Calories from Fat 120	
		%Daily Value*
Total Fat 13g		**20%**
Saturated Fat 4g		**20%**
Trans Fat 0g		
Cholesterol 0mg		**0%**
Sodium 75mg		**3%**
Total Carbohydrate 19g		**6%**
Dietary Fiber 6g		**24%**
Sugars 5g		
Protein 16g		
Vitamin A 25%	•	Vitamin C 6%
Calcium 15%	•	Iron 15%

FUN PROTEIN FACT
After exercise, eating a combination of carbohydrates and protein can help provide a speedy recovery!
It is recommended to consume ~15-25 grams within 30 minutes of exercise!

MILLIONAIRE'S PROTEIN BARS

Yield: 12 Protein Bars

PROTEIN BARS

128g (½ cup) Roasted Almond Butter (Roasted Cashew Butter works great too!)
1 cup + 2 tablespoons Unsweetened Vanilla Almond Milk
1 teaspoon Vanilla Bean Paste
1 teaspoon Vanilla Crème-Flavored Liquid Stevia Extract
90g (¾ cup) Oat Flour
84g (⅔ cup, packed) Vanilla Brown Rice Protein Powder
84g (⅔ cup, packed) Chocolate Brown Rice Protein Powder (you can swap the Chocolate with more Vanilla if you like)
¼ teaspoon Flaked Sea Salt

SALTED CARAMEL FROSTING

105g (⅓ cup) Organic Caramel Sauce (see Pantry Staples on pg. ix)
75g (½ cup, packed) Vanilla Brown Rice Protein Powder
⅛ teaspoon Flaked Sea Salt

CHOCOLATE COATING

6oz Bittersweet Chocolate (70% cacao), melted

FOR THE PROTEIN BARS

① Line an 8x8" brownie pan with parchment paper. Set aside.
② In an electric stand mixer bowl fitted with a beater attachment, add all of the ingredients. Mix on low speed until everything is fully incorporated.
③ Scrape down the sides of the bowl. Mix on medium speed for one last mix. Mixture should be thick and fudgy, like cookie dough.
④ Scoop the mixture into the brownie pan and flatten it out.

FOR THE SALTED CARAMEL FROSTING

⑤ In a small bowl, stir together the caramel sauce, protein powder and salt. Mixture should be thick and slightly sticky. Spoon the mixture over the protein bar base and spread to the edges of the pan. Place in the freezer uncovered for 1 hour.
⑥ Lift the mixture out of the pan. Slice into 12 bars.

Nutrition Facts	
Serving Size 1 Millionaire's Protein Bar (84g)	
Amount Per Serving	
Calories 260	Calories from Fat 110
	%Daily Value*
Total Fat 12g	**18%**
Saturated Fat 4g	**21%**
Trans Fat 0g	
Cholesterol 0mg	**0%**
Sodium 140mg	**6%**
Total Carbohydrate 25g	**8%**
Dietary Fiber 6g	**22%**
Sugars 12g	
Protein 19g	
Vitamin A 0% •	Vitamin C 0%
Calcium 10% •	Iron 15%

FOR THE CHOCOLATE COATING

⑦ Place a silicone baking mat on top of a jelly roll pan and line the protein bars on top. With a large spoon, ladle the melted chocolate over the protein bars. Try to encase the entire bar with chocolate. Feel free to top the bars with a sprinkle of flaked sea salt for decoration!

⑧ Refrigerate until firm (~1 hour). Individually wrap the protein bars in plastic sandwich baggies and refrigerate to store (keeps for ~1 week).

Rich, chocolatey, and caramelly (nope, that's not a word, but that's okay) with a hint of salt. These **MILLIONAIRE'S DIY PROTEIN BARS** will make you feel like royalty!

SCOTCHEROOS PROTEIN BARS

Yield: 15 Scotcheroos

SCOTCHEROOS
120g (4 cups) Crispy Brown Rice Cereal
168g (½ cup) Honey
128g (½ cup) Natural Roasted Peanut Butter
1 teaspoon Natural Butterscotch Flavor
¼ teaspoon Salt
64g (⅔ cup) Vanilla Whey Protein Powder

CHOCOLATE TOPPING
3oz Bittersweet Chocolate (70% cacao), melted

FOR THE SCOTCHEROOS
① Line an 8x8" brownie pan with parchment paper. Set aside.
② In a medium-sized mixing bowl, add the crispy brown rice cereal.
③ In a large microwave-safe bowl, stir together the honey, peanut butter, butterscotch flavor and salt. Microwave at 10-second intervals, stirring between each one, until the mixture is runny and warm. Stir in the protein powder.
④ Fold in the crispy brown rice cereal. When everything is fully incorporated, scoop the mixture into the brownie pan and flatten it out with the silicone spatula. Be sure to press it down so you get a nice and compact cereal treat.

FOR THE CHOCOLATE TOPPING
⑤ Pour the melted chocolate over the base and tilt the pan around until the chocolate covers the entire surface. Tap the pan on the counter a few times to set the chocolate and get rid of any air bubbles. Refrigerate until firm (~1 hour).
⑥ Lift the mixture out of the pan. Slice into 15 bars (5 slices x 3 slices). Store in a tightly sealed container in the fridge with each treat placed on a square of parchment paper to prevent them from sticking (keeps for ~1 week).

Nutrition Facts	
Serving Size 1 Scotcheroo (38g)	
Amount Per Serving	
Calories 170	Calories from Fat 60
	%Daily Value*
Total Fat 7g	11%
Saturated Fat 2g	10%
Trans Fat 0g	
Cholesterol < 5mg	1%
Sodium 90mg	4%
Total Carbohydrate 20.5g	7%
Dietary Fiber 1g	4%
Sugars 10.5g	
Protein 6g	
Vitamin A 0% • Vitamin C 0%	
Calcium 2% • Iron 4%	

ELVIS PROTEIN BARS

Yield: 10 Protein Bars

128g (½ cup) Natural Roasted Peanut Butter
1 cup Unsweetened Vanilla Almond Milk
1 teaspoon Vanilla Crème-Flavored Liquid Stevia Extract
1 teaspoon Banana Flavor
168g (1¼ cups, lightly packed) Vanilla Brown Rice Protein Powder
2oz (1¼ cups) Freeze-Dried Bananas
40g (⅓ cup) Oat Flour
¼ teaspoon Salt

Nutrition Facts	
Serving Size 1 Elvis Protein Bar (64g)	
Amount Per Serving	
Calories 180	Calories from Fat 60
	%Daily Value*
Total Fat 7g	**11%**
Saturated Fat 0.5g	**3%**
Trans Fat 0g	
Cholesterol 0mg	**0%**
Sodium 120mg	**5%**
Total Carbohydrate 14g	**5%**
Dietary Fiber 3g	**14%**
Sugars 5g	
Protein 15g	
Vitamin A 0% • Vitamin C 0%	
Calcium 6% • Iron 10%	

① Line an 8x8" brownie pan with parchment paper. Set aside.
② In an electric stand mixer bowl fitted with a beater attachment, add all of the ingredients. Mix on low speed until everything is fully incorporated. Feel free to add ¼ cup of chopped peanuts!
③ Scrape down the sides of the bowl. Mix on medium speed for one last mix. Mixture should be thick and fudgy, like cookie dough, but with small chunks of banana throughout.
④ Scoop the mixture into the brownie pan and flatten it out. Tightly cover the pan with plastic wrap and refrigerate overnight.
⑤ Lift the mixture out of the pan. Slice into 10 bars. Individually wrap the protein bars in plastic sandwich baggies and refrigerate to store (keeps for ~5 days).

PEANUT BUTTA & JELLY PROTEIN BARS

Yield: 10 Protein Bars

128g (½ cup) Natural Roasted Peanut Butter
1 cup + 2 tablespoons Unsweetened Vanilla Almond Milk
¾ teaspoon Vanilla Crème-Flavored Liquid Stevia Extract
168g (1¼ cups, lightly packed) Vanilla Brown Rice Protein Powder
80g (⅔ cup) Oat Flour
¼ teaspoon Salt
10 teaspoons 100% Fruit Strawberry Spread (or flavor of your choice!)
¼ cup Peanuts, chopped

Nutrition Facts	
Serving Size 1 Peanut Butter & Jelly Protein Bar (76g)	
Amount Per Serving	
Calories 210	Calories from Fat 80
	%Daily Value*
Total Fat 9g	**14%**
Saturated Fat 1.5g	**8%**
Trans Fat 0g	
Cholesterol 0mg	**0%**
Sodium 130mg	**5%**
Total Carbohydrate 16g	**5%**
Dietary Fiber 4g	**14%**
Sugars 5g	
Protein 17g	
Vitamin A 0% • Vitamin C 0%	
Calcium 10% • Iron 15%	

① Line an 8x8" brownie pan with parchment paper. Set aside.
② In an electric stand mixer bowl fitted with a beater attachment, add the peanut butter, almond milk and stevia extract. Mix on low speed while you prepare the dry ingredients.
③ In a medium-sized mixing bowl, whisk together the protein powder, oat flour and salt. Turn off the stand mixer and dump in the dry ingredients. Return mixer to low speed and mix until the dry ingredients are fully incorporated. Scrape down the sides of the bowl if necessary. Mixture should be thick and fudgy, like cookie dough.
④ Scoop the mixture into the brownie pan and flatten it out. Tightly cover the pan with plastic wrap and refrigerate overnight.
⑤ Lift the mixture out of the pan. Slice into 10 bars. Spread the fruit spread over the protein bars (1 teaspoon for each bar) and sprinkle the chopped peanuts on top. To store, simply place a sheet of parchment paper on top of a cake pedestal, arrange the protein bars on top, and cover with a cake dome (keeps for ~1 week).

MATCHA GREEN TEA ALMOND PROTEIN BARS

Yield: 10 Protein Bars

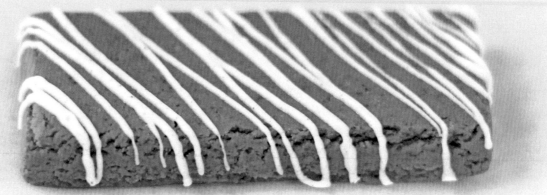

128g (½ cup) Roasted Almond Butter
1 cup Unsweetened Vanilla Almond Milk
1 teaspoon Vanilla Crème-Flavored Liquid Stevia Extract
½ teaspoon Almond Extract
168g (1¼ cups, lightly packed) Vanilla Brown Rice Protein Powder
40g (⅓ cup) Oat Flour
5 teaspoons Matcha Powder
⅛ teaspoon Salt
1oz White Chocolate, melted

Nutrition Facts		
Serving Size 1 Matcha Green Tea Almond Fudge Protein Bar (63g)		
Amount Per Serving		
Calories 170	Calories from Fat 70	
		%Daily Value*
Total Fat 8g		12%
Saturated Fat 1g		5%
Trans Fat 0g		
Cholesterol 0mg		0%
Sodium 90mg		4%
Total Carbohydrate 10g		3%
Dietary Fiber 4g		14%
Sugars 2g		
Protein 16g		
Vitamin A 0%	•	Vitamin C 0%
Calcium 10%	•	Iron 10%

① Line an 8x8" brownie pan with parchment paper. Set aside.
② In an electric stand mixer bowl fitted with a beater attachment, add all of the ingredients except for the white chocolate. Mix on low speed until everything is fully incorporated.
③ Scrape down the sides of the bowl. Mix on medium speed for one last mix. Mixture should be thick and fudgy, like cookie dough.
④ Scoop the mixture into the brownie pan and flatten it out. Tightly cover the pan with plastic wrap and refrigerate overnight.
⑤ Lift the mixture out of the pan. Slice into 10 bars. Drizzle the melted white chocolate over the bars. Refrigerate until firm (~30 minutes).
⑥ Individually wrap the protein bars in plastic sandwich baggies and refrigerate to store (keeps for ~1 week).

SUPER GREENS PROTEIN BARS

Yield: 10 Protein Bars

128g (½ cup) Raw Almond Butter
1 cup + 2 tablespoons Unsweetened Vanilla Almond Milk
1 teaspoon Vanilla Crème-Flavored Liquid Stevia Extract
40 drops Alcohol-Free Liquid Chlorophyll Concentrate (optional, it's just for color)
168g (1¼ cups, lightly packed) Vanilla Brown Rice Protein Powder
60g (½ cup) Oat Flour
50g (⅓ cup, packed) Original Amazing Grass® Amazing Meal® Powder
⅛ teaspoon Salt
¼ cup Mini Semi-Sweet Chocolate Chips or Cacao Nibs

① Line an 8x8" brownie pan with parchment paper. Set aside.
② In an electric stand mixer bowl fitted with a beater attachment, add the almond butter, almond milk, stevia extract and optional liquid chlorophyll. Mix on low speed while you prepare the dry ingredients.
③ In a medium-sized mixing bowl, whisk together the protein powder, oat flour, Amazing Grass® powder and salt. Turn off the stand mixer and dump in the dry ingredients. Return mixer to low speed and mix until the dry ingredients are fully incorporated. Scrape down the sides of the bowl if necessary. Mixture should be thick and fudgy, like cookie dough.
④ Scoop the mixture into the brownie pan and flatten it out. Sprinkle the mini chocolate chips or cacao nibs on top and press them into the surface. Tightly cover the pan with plastic wrap and refrigerate overnight.
⑤ Lift the mixture out of the pan. Slice into 10 bars. Individually wrap the protein bars in plastic sandwich baggies and refrigerate to store (keeps for ~5 days).

Nutrition Facts		
Serving Size 1 Super Greens Fudge Protein Bar (73g)		
Amount Per Serving		
Calories 210		Calories from Fat 80
		%Daily Value*
Total Fat 9g		**14%**
Saturated Fat 1.5g		**7%**
Trans Fat 0g		
Cholesterol 0mg		**0%**
Sodium 90mg		**4%**
Total Carbohydrate 15g		**5%**
Dietary Fiber 5g		**20%**
Sugars 3g		
Protein 19g		
Vitamin A 20%	•	Vitamin C 10%
Calcium 15%	•	Iron 20%

CHUBBY HUBBY PROTEIN BARS
(pg. 71-72)

CANDY BAR FLAVORS

PUMPED UP PROTEIN BARS
A Healthier Version of Milky Way®

Yield: 12 Protein Bars

PROTEIN BARS
128g (½ cup) Roasted Almond Butter
1 cup + 2 tablespoons Unsweetened Vanilla Almond Milk
1 teaspoon Vanilla Crème-Flavored Liquid Stevia Extract
168g (1¼ cups, lightly packed) Chocolate Brown Rice Protein Powder
80g (⅔ cup) Oat Flour
¼ teaspoon Salt

CARAMEL LAYER
105g (⅓ cup) Organic Caramel Sauce (see Pantry Staples on pg. ix)
63g (½ cup, lightly packed) Vanilla Brown Rice Protein Powder

CHOCOLATE-ALMOND COATING
6oz Milk Chocolate with Salted Almonds, melted
1 tablespoon Coconut Oil, melted

FOR THE PROTEIN BARS
① Line an 8x8" brownie pan with parchment paper. Set aside.
② In an electric stand mixer bowl fitted with a beater attachment, add the almond butter, almond milk and stevia extract. Mix on low speed while you prepare the dry ingredients.
③ In a medium-sized mixing bowl, whisk together the protein powder, oat flour and salt. Turn off the stand mixer and dump in the dry ingredients. Return mixer to low speed and mix until the dry ingredients are fully incorporated. Scrape down the sides of the bowl if necessary. Mixture should be thick and fudgy, like cookie dough.
④ Scoop the mixture into the brownie pan and flatten it out.

FOR THE CARAMEL LAYER
⑤ In a small bowl, stir together the caramel sauce and protein powder. Mixture should be thick and slightly sticky. Spoon the mixture over the protein bar base and spread to the edges of the pan. Place in the freezer uncovered for 1 hour.
⑥ Lift the mixture out of the pan. Slice into 12 bars.

FOR THE CHOCOLATE-ALMOND COATING

⑦ Stir the coconut oil into the melted chocolate.

⑧ Place a silicone baking mat on top of a jelly roll pan and line the protein bars on top. With a large spoon, ladle the melted chocolate over the protein bars. Try to encase the entire bar with chocolate.

⑨ Refrigerate until firm (~1 hour). Individually wrap the protein bars in plastic sandwich baggies and refrigerate to store (keeps for ~1 week).

Nutrition Facts	
Serving Size 1 Pumped Up Protein Bar (83g)	

Amount Per Serving	
Calories 280	Calories from Fat 100

	%Daily Value*
Total Fat 12.5g	18%
Saturated Fat 4.5g	18%
Trans Fat 0g	
Cholesterol 0mg	1%
Sodium 140mg	6%
Total Carbohydrate 23g	8%
Dietary Fiber 4g	17%
Sugars 13g	
Protein 19g	

Vitamin A 0%	•	Vitamin C 0%
Calcium 15%	•	Iron 20%

FUN PROTEIN FACT

Peanut butter, almond butter, oats, garbanzo beans!

They are all high in protein, but they are *incomplete* proteins. This means that they don't contain all the essential amino acids necessary for muscle growth, repair and maintenance. These foods need to be paired with *complementary proteins* – proteins that contain those missing amino acids.

For example, in this Pumped Up Protein Bar recipe, you will get a complete protein because the almond butter and oat flour "complement" each other. Together, they contain the essential amino acids you need!

Milky Way® is a registered trademark of Mars, Inc. Mars, Inc. is not related in any way to Desserts with Benefits, Inc.

SHREDDED PROTEIN BARS

A Healthier Version of Twix®

Yield: 12 Protein Bars

PROTEIN BARS
128g (½ cup) Roasted Almond Butter
1 cup Unsweetened Vanilla Almond Milk
1 teaspoon Vanilla Crème-Flavored Liquid Stevia Extract
½ teaspoon Natural Butter Flavor
168g (1¼ cups, lightly packed) Vanilla Brown Rice Protein Powder
80g (⅔ cup) Oat Flour
¼ teaspoon Salt

CARAMEL LAYER
105g (⅓ cup) Organic Caramel Sauce (see Pantry Staples on pg. ix)
63g (½ cup, lightly packed) Vanilla Brown Rice Protein Powder

CHOCOLATE COATING
6oz Milk Chocolate (34% cacao), melted
1 tablespoon Coconut Oil, melted

FOR THE PROTEIN BARS
① Line an 8x8" brownie pan with parchment paper. Set aside.
② In an electric stand mixer bowl fitted with a beater attachment, add all of the ingredients. Mix on low speed until everything is fully incorporated.
③ Scrape down the sides of the bowl. Mix on medium speed for one last mix. Mixture should be thick and fudgy, like cookie dough.
④ Scoop the mixture into the brownie pan and flatten it out.

FOR THE CARAMEL LAYER
⑤ In a small bowl, stir together the caramel sauce and protein powder. Mixture should be thick and slightly sticky. Spoon the mixture over the protein bar base and spread to the edges of the pan (I used an offset spatula). Place in the freezer uncovered for 1 hour.
⑥ Lift the mixture out of the pan. Slice into 12 bars.

Nutrition Facts	
Serving Size 1 Shredded Protein Bar (81g)	
Amount Per Serving	
Calories 270	Calories from Fat 110
	%Daily Value*
Total Fat 12g	**18%**
Saturated Fat 4.5g	**22%**
Trans Fat 0g	
Cholesterol < 5mg	**1%**
Sodium 125mg	**5%**
Total Carbohydrate 25g	**8%**
Dietary Fiber 4g	**16%**
Sugars 14g	
Protein 19g	
Vitamin A 0%	Vitamin C 0%
Calcium 10%	Iron 15%

FOR THE CHOCOLATE COATING

⑦ Stir the coconut oil into the melted chocolate.

⑧ Place a silicone baking mat on top of a jelly roll pan and line the protein bars on top. With a large spoon, ladle the melted chocolate over the protein bars. Try to encase the entire bar with chocolate.

⑨ Refrigerate until firm (~1 hour). Individually wrap the protein bars in plastic sandwich baggies and refrigerate to store (keeps for ~1 week).

Twix® is a registered trademark of Mars, Inc. Mars, Inc. is not related in any way to Desserts with Benefits, Inc.

BEEFCAKE PROTEIN BARS

A Healthier Version of Snickers®

Yield: 12 Protein Bars

PROTEIN BARS

128g (½ cup) Natural Roasted Peanut Butter
1 cup + 2 tablespoons Unsweetened Vanilla Almond Milk
1 teaspoon Vanilla Crème-Flavored Liquid Stevia Extract
168g (1¼ cups, lightly packed) Vanilla Brown Rice Protein Powder
80g (⅔ cup) Oat Flour
¼ teaspoon Salt

CARAMEL LAYER

105g (⅓ cup) Organic Caramel Sauce (see Pantry Staples on pg. ix)
63g (½ cup, lightly packed) Vanilla Brown Rice Protein Powder
¼ cup Peanuts

CHOCOLATE COATING

6oz Milk Chocolate (34% cacao), melted
1 tablespoon Coconut Oil, melted

FOR THE PROTEIN BARS

① Line an 8x8" brownie pan with parchment paper. Set aside.
② In an electric stand mixer bowl fitted with a beater attachment, add the peanut butter, almond milk and stevia extract. Mix on low speed while you prepare the dry ingredients.
③ In a medium-sized mixing bowl, whisk together the protein powder, oat flour and salt. Turn off the stand mixer and dump in the dry ingredients. Return mixer to low speed and mix until the dry ingredients are fully incorporated. Scrape down the sides of the bowl if necessary. Mixture should be thick and fudgy, like cookie dough.
④ Scoop the mixture into the brownie pan and flatten it out.

FOR THE CARAMEL LAYER

⑤ In a small bowl, stir together the caramel sauce and protein powder. Mixture should be thick and slightly sticky. Spoon the mixture over the protein bar base and spread to the edges of the pan. Sprinkle the chopped peanuts on top and press them into the surface. Place in the freezer uncovered for 1 hour.

⑥ Lift the mixture out of the pan. Slice into 12 bars.

FOR THE CHOCOLATE COATING

⑦ Stir the coconut oil into the melted chocolate.

⑧ Place a silicone baking mat on top of a jelly roll pan and line the protein bars on top. With a large spoon, ladle the melted chocolate over the protein bars. Try to encase the entire bar with chocolate.

⑨ Refrigerate until firm (~1 hour). Individually wrap the protein bars in plastic sandwich baggies and refrigerate to store (keeps for ~1 week).

Nutrition Facts	
Serving Size 1 Beefcake Protein Bar (84g)	

Amount Per Serving	
Calories 280	Calories from Fat 110

	%Daily Value*
Total Fat 12g	**18%**
Saturated Fat 4.5g	**22%**
Trans Fat 0g	
Cholesterol < 5mg	**1%**
Sodium 130mg	**5%**
Total Carbohydrate 25g	**8%**
Dietary Fiber 4g	**14%**
Sugars 14g	
Protein 18g	

Vitamin A 0%	•	Vitamin C 0%
Calcium 8%	•	Iron 15%

Snickers® is a registered trademark of Mars, Inc. Mars, Inc. is not related in any way to Desserts with Benefits, Inc.

IN THE BUFF PROTEIN BARS

A Healthier Version of Reese's®

Yield: 10 Protein Bars

PROTEIN BARS
128g (½ cup) Natural Roasted Peanut Butter
1 cup + 2 tablespoons Unsweetened Vanilla Almond Milk
1 teaspoon Vanilla Crème-Flavored Liquid Stevia Extract
168g (1¼ cups, lightly packed) Vanilla Brown Rice Protein Powder
80g (⅔ cup) Oat Flour
¼ teaspoon Salt

CHOCOLATE COATING
6oz Milk Chocolate (34% cacao), melted

FOR THE PROTEIN BARS
① Line an 8x8" brownie pan with parchment paper. Set aside.
② In an electric stand mixer bowl fitted with a beater attachment, add the peanut butter, almond milk and stevia extract. Mix on low speed while you prepare the dry ingredients.
③ In a medium-sized mixing bowl, whisk together the protein powder, oat flour and salt. Turn off the stand mixer and dump in the dry ingredients. Return mixer to low speed and mix until the dry ingredients are fully incorporated. Scrape down the sides of the bowl if necessary. Mixture should be thick and fudgy, like cookie dough.
④ Scoop the mixture into the brownie pan and flatten it out. Tightly cover the pan with plastic wrap and refrigerate overnight.
⑤ Lift the mixture out of the pan. Slice into 10 bars.

FOR THE CHOCOLATE COATING
⑥ Place a silicone baking mat on top of a jelly roll pan and line the protein bars on top. With a large spoon, ladle the melted chocolate over the protein bars. Try to encase the entire bar with chocolate, but it doesn't have to be perfect.
⑦ Refrigerate until firm (~1 hour). Individually wrap the protein bars in plastic sandwich baggies and refrigerate to store (keeps for ~1 week).

Nutrition Facts

Serving Size 1 In The Buff Protein Bar (82g)

Amount Per Serving

Calories 270	Calories from Fat 110

	%Daily Value*
Total Fat 13g	**20%**
Saturated Fat 4g	**20%**
Trans Fat 0g	
Cholesterol < 5mg	**1%**
Sodium 135mg	**6%**
Total Carbohydrate 21g	**7%**
Dietary Fiber 4g	**15%**
Sugars 10g	
Protein 18g	

Vitamin A 0%	•	Vitamin C 0%
Calcium 10%	•	Iron 15%

These **IN THE BUFF DIY PROTEIN BARS** will make you feel naughty.

You'll wanna get in the buff!

Reese's® is a registered trademark of The Hershey Company. The Hershey Company is not related in any way to Desserts with Benefits, Inc.

LET'S RACE PROTEIN BARS

A Healthier Version of Take5®

Yield: 12 Protein Bars

PROTEIN BARS

128g (½ cup) Natural Roasted Peanut Butter
1 cup + 3 tablespoons Unsweetened Vanilla Almond Milk
1 teaspoon Vanilla Crème-Flavored Liquid Stevia Extract
168g (1¼ cups, lightly packed) Vanilla Brown Rice Protein Powder
90g (¾ cup) Peanut Flour
¼ teaspoon Salt

TOPPINGS

105g (⅓ cup) Organic Caramel Sauce (see Pantry Staples on pg. ix)
40g (⅓ cup) Peanut Flour
24 Pretzel Rods
¼ cup Peanuts

CHOCOLATE COATING

6oz Bittersweet Chocolate (70% cacao), melted

FOR THE PROTEIN BARS

① Line an 8x8" brownie pan with parchment paper. Set aside.
② In an electric stand mixer bowl fitted with a beater attachment, add all of the ingredients. Mix on low speed until everything is fully incorporated.
③ Scrape down the sides of the bowl. Mix on medium speed for one last mix. Mixture should be thick and fudgy, like cookie dough.
④ Scoop the mixture into the brownie pan and flatten it out.

FOR THE TOPPINGS

⑤ In a small bowl, stir together the caramel sauce and peanut flour. Mixture should be thick and slightly sticky. Spoon the mixture over the protein bar base and spread to the edges of the pan. Place in the freezer uncovered for 2 hours.
⑥ Lift the mixture out of the pan. Slice into 12 bars.
⑦ Press the pretzel rods (2 rods per bar) and peanuts into the caramel.

Take5® is a registered trademark of The Hershey Company. The Hershey Company is not related in any way to Desserts with Benefits, Inc.

FOR THE CHOCOLATE COATING

⑧ Place a silicone baking mat on top of a jelly roll pan and line the protein bars on top. With a large spoon, ladle the melted chocolate over the protein bars. Try to encase the entire bar with chocolate.

⑨ Refrigerate until firm (~2 hours). Individually wrap the protein bars in plastic sandwich baggies and refrigerate to store (keeps for ~1 week, but the pretzels will be at their crunchiest for the first couple of days).

Chewy, crunchy, sweet, and salty.
One bite of these
LET'S RACE DIY PROTEIN BARS
and you'll shoot straight up into
delicious, healthy dessert nirvana!

Nutrition Facts		
Serving Size 1 Let's Race Protein Bar (95g)		
Amount Per Serving		
Calories 330	Calories from Fat 140	
		%Daily Value*
Total Fat 15g		**23%**
Saturated Fat 4.5g		**23%**
Trans Fat 0g		
Cholesterol 0mg		**0%**
Sodium 220mg		**9%**
Total Carbohydrate 29g		**10%**
Dietary Fiber 6g		**24%**
Sugars 12g		
Protein 21g		
Vitamin A 0%	•	Vitamin C 0%
Calcium 8%	•	Iron 20%

CHUBBY HUBBY PROTEIN BARS

Yield: 12 Protein Bars

PROTEIN BARS

128g (½ cup) Natural Roasted Peanut Butter
1 cup + 3 tablespoons Unsweetened Vanilla Almond Milk
1 teaspoon Vanilla Crème-Flavored Liquid Stevia Extract
168g (1¼ cups, lightly packed) Vanilla Brown Rice Protein Powder
90g (¾ cup) Peanut Flour
¼ teaspoon Salt

TOPPINGS

3oz Bittersweet Chocolate (70% cacao), melted
36 Pretzel Rods

FOR THE PROTEIN BARS

① Line an 8x8" brownie pan with parchment paper. Set aside.
② In an electric stand mixer bowl fitted with a beater attachment, add all of the ingredients. Mix on low speed until everything is fully incorporated.
③ Scrape down the sides of the bowl. Mix on medium speed for one last mix. Mixture should be thick and fudgy, like cookie dough.
④ Scoop the mixture into the brownie pan and flatten it out. Tightly cover the pan with plastic wrap and refrigerate overnight.
⑤ Lift the mixture out of the pan. Slice into 12 bars.

FOR THE TOPPINGS

⑥ Place a silicone baking mat on top of a jelly roll pan and line the protein bars on top. Spread just a little bit of melted chocolate over a protein bar, then press 3 pretzel rods on top so they adhere as the chocolate firms up. Do this with the rest of the protein bars. Drizzle the remaining chocolate over the protein bars.
⑦ Refrigerate until firm (~1 hour). Individually wrap the protein bars in plastic sandwich baggies and refrigerate to store (keeps for ~1 week).

Nutrition Facts	
Serving Size 1 Chubby Hubby Protein Bar (78g)	
Amount Per Serving	
Calories 250	Calories from Fat 90
	%Daily Value*
Total Fat 10.5g	**16%**
Saturated Fat 2.5g	**13%**
Trans Fat 0g	
Cholesterol 0mg	**0%**
Sodium 270mg	**11%**
Total Carbohydrate 21g	**7%**
Dietary Fiber 5g	**20%**
Sugars 4g	
Protein 18g	
Vitamin A 0%	Vitamin C 0%
Calcium 6%	Iron 15%

POWERHOUSE PROTEIN BARS

A Healthier Version of Payday®

Yield: 24 Protein Bars

160g (½ cup) Organic Caramel Sauce (see Pantry Staples on pg. ix)
128g (½ cup) Natural Roasted Peanut Butter
1 cup Unsweetened Vanilla Almond Milk
1 teaspoon Vanilla Crème-Flavored Liquid Stevia Extract
147g (1 cup, packed) Vanilla Brown Rice Protein Powder
120g (1 cup) Peanut Flour
⅛ teaspoon Salt
12oz (3 cups) Peanuts

① Line an 8x8" brownie pan with parchment paper. Set aside.
② In an electric stand mixer bowl fitted with a beater attachment, add the caramel sauce, peanut butter, almond milk and stevia extract. Mix on low speed while you prepare the dry ingredients.
③ In a medium-sized mixing bowl, whisk together the protein powder, peanut flour and salt. Turn off the stand mixer and dump in the dry ingredients. Return mixer to low speed and mix until the dry ingredients are fully incorporated. Scrape down the sides of the bowl if necessary. Mixture should be thick, fudgy, and slightly sticky, like a wet cookie dough.
④ Scoop the mixture into the brownie pan and flatten it out. Place in the freezer for 1 hour.
⑤ Lift the mixture out of the pan. Slice into 12 bars, then slice each bar in half lengthwise so you get 24 strips.
⑥ Add the peanuts to a large dish. Press the protein strips into the peanuts to coat the strips entirely. Roll each strip a few times to round out the edges and get the peanuts to adhere completely. Individually wrap the protein bars in plastic sandwich baggies and refrigerate to store (keeps for ~1 week).

Nutrition Facts

Serving Size 1 Powerhouse Protein Bar (48g)

Amount Per Serving

Calories 170   Calories from Fat 90

	%Daily Value*
Total Fat 11g	**16%**
Saturated Fat 1.5g	**7%**
Trans Fat 0g	
Cholesterol 0mg	**0%**
Sodium 40mg	**2%**
Total Carbohydrate 12g	**4%**
Dietary Fiber 3g	**11%**
Sugars 6g	
Protein 12g	

Vitamin A 0%	•	Vitamin C 0%	
Calcium 6%	•	Iron 6%	

Peanut butter lovers, REJOICE! These
POWERHOUSE DIY PROTEIN BARS
are packed with 3 peanutty components.
They will restore your faith in everything!

PayDay® is a registered trademark of The Hershey Company. The Hershey Company is not related in any way to Desserts with Benefits, Inc.

DYNAMIC PROTEIN BARS

A Healthier Version of Mounds®

Yield: 12 Protein Bars

PROTEIN BARS
128g (½ cup) Raw Coconut Butter, melted
1 cup + 2 tablespoons Unsweetened Vanilla Coconut Milk, room temperature
1 teaspoon Coconut-Flavored Liquid Stevia Extract
168g (1¼ cups, lightly packed) Vanilla Brown Rice Protein Powder
36g (¼ cup) Coconut Flour
⅛ teaspoon Salt

CHOCOLATE-COCONUT COATING
6oz Bittersweet Chocolate (70% cacao), melted
64g (¼ cup) Raw Coconut Butter

FOR THE PROTEIN BARS
① Line an 8x8" brownie pan with parchment paper. Set aside.
② In an electric stand mixer bowl fitted with a beater attachment, add the melted coconut butter, coconut milk and stevia extract. Mix on low speed while you prepare the dry ingredients.
③ In a medium-sized mixing bowl, whisk together the protein powder, coconut flour and salt. Turn off the stand mixer and dump in the dry ingredients. Return mixer to low speed and mix until the dry ingredients are fully incorporated. Scrape down the sides of the bowl if necessary. Mixture should be thick and fudgy, like cookie dough.
④ Scoop the mixture into the brownie pan and flatten it out. Tightly cover the pan with plastic wrap and refrigerate overnight.
⑤ Lift the mixture out of the pan and let it sit on the counter for 10 minutes to soften. Slice into 12 bars.

FOR THE CHOCOLATE-COCONUT COATING
⑥ Stir the coconut butter into the melted chocolate.
⑦ Place a silicone baking mat on top of a jelly roll pan and line the protein bars on top. With a large spoon, ladle the melted chocolate over the protein bars. Try to encase the entire bar with chocolate, but it doesn't have to be perfect.
⑧ Refrigerate until firm (~1 hour). Individually wrap the protein bars in plastic sandwich baggies and refrigerate to store (keeps for ~1 week).

Nutrition Facts

Serving Size 1 Dynamic Protein Bar (70g)

Amount Per Serving

Calories 230 Calories from Fat 140

%Daily Value*

Total Fat 15g	**23%**
Saturated Fat 12g	**61%**
Trans Fat 0g	
Cholesterol 0mg	**0%**
Sodium 70mg	**3%**
Total Carbohydrate 14g	**5%**
Dietary Fiber 7g	**26%**
Sugars 7g	
Protein 13g	

Vitamin A 0%	•	Vitamin C 0%
Calcium 6%	•	Iron 15%

You put the ~~lime~~ chocolate on the coconut and you'll eat these

DYNAMIC DIY PROTEIN BARS

all up!

Mounds® is a registered trademark of The Hershey Company. The Hershey Company is not related in any way to Desserts with Benefits, Inc.

DUO PROTEIN BARS

A Healthier Version of Almond Joy®

Yield: 12 Protein Bars

PROTEIN BARS

96g (6 tablespoons) Raw Coconut Butter, melted
1 cup + 2 tablespoons Unsweetened Vanilla Coconut Milk, room temperature
1 teaspoon Coconut-Flavored Liquid Stevia Extract
1 teaspoon Almond Extract
168g (1 ¼ cups, lightly packed) Vanilla Brown Rice Protein Powder
36g (¼ cup) Coconut Flour
⅛ teaspoon Salt
48 Whole Almonds

CHOCOLATE-COCONUT COATING

6oz Bittersweet Chocolate (70% cacao), melted
64g (¼ cup) Raw Coconut Butter

FOR THE PROTEIN BARS

① Line an 8x8" brownie pan with parchment paper. Set aside.
② In an electric stand mixer bowl fitted with a beater attachment, add the melted coconut butter, coconut milk, stevia extract and almond extract. Mix on low speed while you prepare the dry ingredients.
③ In a medium-sized mixing bowl, whisk together the protein powder, coconut flour and salt. Turn off the stand mixer and dump in the dry ingredients. Return mixer to low speed and mix until the dry ingredients are fully incorporated. Scrape down the sides of the bowl if necessary. Mixture should be thick and fudgy, like cookie dough.
④ Scoop the mixture into the brownie pan and flatten it out. Tightly cover the pan with plastic wrap and refrigerate overnight.
⑤ Lift the mixture out of the pan and let it sit on the counter for 10 minutes to soften. Slice into 12 bars. Press 4-5 almonds on top of each protein bar to make a line of almonds.

FOR THE CHOCOLATE-COCONUT COATING

⑥ Stir the coconut butter into the melted chocolate.
⑦ Place a silicone baking mat on top of a jelly roll pan and line the protein bars on top. With a large spoon, ladle the melted chocolate over the protein bars. Try to encase the entire bar with chocolate, but it doesn't have to be perfect.

⑧ Refrigerate until firm (~1 hour). Individually wrap the protein bars in plastic sandwich baggies and refrigerate to store (keeps for ~1 week).

Super chocolatey and fudgy with some crunch from the almonds, these

DUO DIY PROTEIN BARS

will satisfy even the most insatiable sweet tooth of all!

Nutrition Facts

Serving Size 1 Duo Protein Bar (71g)

Amount Per Serving	
Calories 230	Calories from Fat 140

	%Daily Value*
Total Fat 15g	**24%**
Saturated Fat 10g	**52%**
Trans Fat 0g	
Cholesterol 0mg	**0%**
Sodium 70mg	**3%**
Total Carbohydrate 14g	**5%**
Dietary Fiber 6g	**26%**
Sugars 6g	
Protein 13g	

Vitamin A 0%	•	Vitamin C 0%
Calcium 6%	•	Iron 15%

Almond Joy® is a registered trademark of The Hershey Company. The Hershey Company is not related in any way to Desserts with Benefits, Inc.

I'M SO RIPPED PROTEIN BARS

A Healthier Version of Cherry Ripe®

Yield: 12 Protein Bars

PROTEIN BARS

128g (½ cup) Raw Coconut Butter, melted
1 cup + 2 tablespoons Unsweetened Vanilla Coconut Milk, room temperature
1 teaspoon Coconut-Flavored Liquid Stevia Extract
1 teaspoon Cherry Flavor
2 cups Freeze-Dried Cherries, ground into a coarse powder (measure after grinding)
168g (1¼ cups, lightly packed) Vanilla Brown Rice Protein Powder
⅛ teaspoon Salt

CHOCOLATE-COCONUT COATING

6oz Bittersweet Chocolate (70% cacao), melted
64g (¼ cup) Raw Coconut Butter

FOR THE PROTEIN BARS

① Line an 8x8" brownie pan with parchment paper. Set aside.
② In an electric stand mixer bowl fitted with a beater attachment, add all of the ingredients. Mix on low speed until everything is fully incorporated.
③ Scrape down the sides of the bowl. Mix on medium speed for one last mix. Mixture should be thick and fudgy, like cookie dough.
④ Scoop the mixture into the brownie pan and flatten it out. Tightly cover the pan with plastic wrap and refrigerate overnight.
⑤ Lift the mixture out of the pan. Slice into 12 bars.

FOR THE CHOCOLATE-COCONUT COATING

⑥ Stir the coconut butter into the melted chocolate.
⑦ Place a silicone baking mat on top of a jelly roll pan and line the protein bars on top. With a large spoon, ladle the melted chocolate over the protein bars. Try to encase the entire bar with chocolate, but it doesn't have to be perfect.
⑧ Refrigerate until firm (~1 hour). Individually wrap the protein bars in plastic sandwich baggies and refrigerate to store (keeps for ~1 week).

Nutrition Facts	
Serving Size 1 I'm So Ripped Protein Bar (80g)	
Amount Per Serving	
Calories 300	Calories from Fat 140
	%Daily Value*
Total Fat 15g	**23%**
Saturated Fat 12g	**59%**
Trans Fat 0g	
Cholesterol 0mg	**0%**
Sodium 70mg	**3%**
Total Carbohydrate 27g	**9%**
Dietary Fiber 7g	**22%**
Sugars 19g	
Protein 15g	
Vitamin A 10%	Vitamin C 6%
Calcium 8%	Iron 20%

Cherry Ripe® is a registered trademark of Cadbury, Ltd. Cadbury, Ltd. is not related in any way to Desserts with Benefits, Inc.

THE
ULTIMATE
FLAVOR

A FLAVOR SO GOOD
IT NEEDS ITS
OWN SECTION!

DEATH BY CHOCOLATE PROTEIN BARS

(aka Quintuple Chocolate "Candy" Bars)

Yield: 12 Protein Bars

PROTEIN BARS

128g (½ cup) Roasted Almond Butter
1 cup + 2 tablespoons Unsweetened Vanilla Almond Milk
1 teaspoon Vanilla Crème-Flavored Liquid Stevia Extract
½ teaspoon Natural Butter Flavor
168g (1¼ cups, lightly packed) Chocolate Brown Rice Protein Powder
80g (⅔ cup) Oat Flour
¼ cup Unsweetened Natural Cocoa Powder
¼ teaspoon Salt

CHOCOLATE FROSTING

230g (1 cup) Plain, Nonfat Greek Yogurt
½ teaspoon Natural Butter Flavor
½ teaspoon Vanilla Crème-Flavored Liquid Stevia Extract
2 tablespoons Unsweetened Natural Cocoa Powder
½ teaspoon Psyllium Husk Powder
¼ teaspoon Espresso Powder

CHOCOLATE COATING

6oz Bittersweet Chocolate (70% cacao), melted
¼ cup Mini Semi-Sweet Chocolate Chips

FOR THE PROTEIN BARS

① Line an 8x8" brownie pan with parchment paper. Set aside.
② In an electric stand mixer bowl fitted with a beater attachment, add all of the ingredients. Mix on low speed until everything is fully incorporated.
③ Scrape down the sides of the bowl. Mix on medium speed for one last mix. Mixture should be thick and fudgy, like cookie dough.

Nutrition Facts	
Serving Size 1 Death By Chocolate Protein Bar (94g)	
Amount Per Serving	
Calories 240	Calories from Fat 120
	%Daily Value*
Total Fat 13g	20%
Saturated Fat 5g	25%
Trans Fat 0g	
Cholesterol 0mg	0%
Sodium 100mg	4%
Total Carbohydrate 17g	6%
Dietary Fiber 6g	25%
Sugars 8g	
Protein 18g	
Vitamin A 0%	Vitamin C 0%
Calcium 15%	Iron 25%

④ Scoop the mixture into the brownie pan and flatten it out.

FOR THE CHOCOLATE FROSTING
⑤ In a medium-sized mixing bowl, whisk together the Greek yogurt, butter flavor and stevia extract.
⑥ In a small bowl, whisk together the cocoa powder, psyllium husk powder and espresso powder. Dump the dry ingredients over the wet ingredients and whisk until smooth. Spoon the mixture over the protein bar base and spread to the edges of the pan (I used an offset spatula). Place in the freezer uncovered for 1 hour.
⑦ Lift the mixture out of the pan. Slice into 12 bars.

FOR THE CHOCOLATE COATING
⑧ Place a silicone baking mat on top of a jelly roll pan and line the protein bars on top. With a large spoon, ladle the melted chocolate over the protein bars. Try to encase the entire bar with chocolate. Sprinkle the chocolate chips on top.
⑨ Refrigerate until firm (~1 hour). To store, simply place a sheet of parchment paper on top of a cake pedestal, arrange the protein bars on top, and cover with a cake dome (keeps for ~1 week).

Fudgy.
Rich.
Decadent.
Sweet.
Chocolatey.

If you like dessert (and I sure hope you do), then these
DEATH BY CHOCOLATE DIY PROTEIN BARS
are for you!

REMEMBER...

FOOD = *Love* ♥

40014145R00066

Made in the USA
Middletown, DE
31 January 2017